DELIGHT

yourself in the Lord and He will give you the desires of your heart. ~ Psalm 37:4

What if God meant for you to enjoy his commandments?

PAT
MENSER

WITH DISCUSSION QUESTIONS

Warren Publishing, Inc.

Published by Warren Publishing, Inc.
Charlotte, NC
www.warrenpublishing.net

ISBN: 978-1-943258-02-4

Library of Congress Control Number: 2015935111

Published by Warren Publishing, Inc.
www.warrenpublishing.net

MERCY HAS A SUPERNATURAL EFFECT ON THE TEN COMMANDMENTS,

changing them from laws we're unable to keep, to expressions of God's love written on our hearts and minds. But to accept the beauty of this transformation, we need to understand the difference between The Ten Commandments and the Law of Moses.

The Law of Moses contains over 600 commandments. These laws were *written by Moses on paper.* God told Moses to place these laws *beside* the ark as a witness against the rebellious Israelites (Deuteronomy 31:24-27a). The Law of Moses (also called The Book of the Law) was *temporary*. In time God would nail these external, paper regulations to the cross. Thank God they are gone!

The Ten Commandments, however, are *permanent*. These laws were *written by God in stone*. God told Moses to place these laws *inside* the ark (Deuteronomy 10:1-5). They are physically still there, and intended to be spiritually engraved in our hearts and minds.

> *"This is the covenant I will make with them after that time, says the Lord. I will put my laws in their hearts, and I will write them on their minds." Then he adds: " Their sins and lawless acts I will remember no more." And where these have been forgiven, there is no longer any sacrifice for sin.*
> Hebrews 10:16-18

Apart from God writing his laws in our hearts, we would have neither the desire nor the ability to walk in the path of his commands. But once mercy places these laws inside of us, they become both a light and a delight for us to follow.

Delight leads you on a journey that reclaims the beauty, love and wisdom contained within The Ten Commandments. And as you'll see in chapter eleven, the ride is entirely free!

DEDICATION

For Aaron, John, Michael, Clara, Julia,
and the generations who follow you.

He decreed statutes for Jacob and established the law in Israel,
which he commanded our forefathers to teach their children,
so the next generation would know them,
even the children yet to be born,
and they in turn would tell their children.
Psalm 78:5-6

ACKNOWLEDGEMENTS

Thank you to my parents, the late Paul J. Hinton and Mary Collins, for taking my sisters and me to church when we were growing up. Daddy, you worked in the coal mine and ran a farm; tired and busy you were, yet you made Sundays a special day for our family. Mom, you had three little girls to primp and get ready for Sunday School; you did it and were on time, despite Daddy being the last one in the car. And I remember coming home from church, opening our back door and smelling the aroma of a roast dinner with carrots and potatoes, promising our family a delicious Sunday dinner.

To the late Mildred Vannoy, my fifth- and seventh-grade teacher, thank you for giving me the opportunity to enjoy turning the pages of a bible as you led our class in daily bible drills. And the box full of prizes for the weekly winners you provided from your meager teacher's salary. I honor your dedication to your students and the impact you've had on so many lives.

A lifetime of thanks to Ruth Davis, friend, intercessor, songwriter and musician. You were my first editor. For years we mailed manuscripts back and forth (handwritten), until the framework of *Delight* was formed. You are the epitome of friendship and faithfulness.

To Brenda Hayes, thank you for being you! Together we've kicked a few leaves along life's path. Your grateful heart and content disposition have been an inspiration to me. I count our friendship as one of the sweetest blessings in my life.

Thank you to Kyle Matthews, minister, singer and songwriter, for permission to use your lyrics in Chapter 6. The reader who would like to hear more of Kyle's songs should go to his website, www.kylematthews.com.

And to Mike, my husband of nearly forty years, thank you. Your strong work ethic, faithful support and steady hand have provided me with the time and resources necessary to bring *Delight* to life.

PROLOGUE

Kool-Aid and cookies, making picture frames from popsicle sticks and crafting ashtrays from clay (it was the '60s!), are what drew me to the Ten Commandments. Bible school filled my summers with a child-like wonder of "Who is God?" Even as a young child, I knew God spoke to us through these commandments. I didn't know exactly how, but I instinctively knew that *somehow* these commandments connected us to God.

As decades passed, I often would hear that these commandments were obsolete, done away with, Old Testament teachings that didn't reflect the grace provided for us through the life of Jesus. This sounded like partial truth to me. And though I knew of God's grace, walked in and taught about his grace, I still loved my Kool-Aid commandments. They were near and dear to my heart, and I couldn't believe they were irrelevant to my relationship with Jesus.

I'd been taught that God is love. My simple mindset deduced that if God is love, then there must be love in his commandments. This belief was strengthened when I had children of my own. As a mother, I knew that the values I wanted to impart to my sons were much more than rules for them to follow: they were a reflection of me, my character, and, most important, an expression of my love for them. And so it was from the perspective of God's love for me that I began an earnest study of the Ten Commandments.

I came to see these commandments as multi-faceted in their purpose. For the person searching for God and the pathway to eternal life, the Ten Commandments are meant to define sin and actually to magnify our inability to keep these commandments in order to show us our need for a Savior.

So the law was put in charge to lead us to Christ
that we might be justified by faith.
Galatians 3:24

But for we who have been justified by Christ, those once external laws are engraved in our hearts and on our minds. We now have an intimate, *internal* relationship with God and his laws.

"This is the covenant I will make with them after that time, says the Lord.
I will put my laws in their hearts, and I will write them on their minds."
Then he adds: "Their sins and lawless acts I will remember no more."
And where these have been forgiven, there is no longer any sacrifice for sin.
Hebrews 10:16–18

With God's commandments actually written in our hearts and on our minds, God's desires literally become our desires. Christ in us wants to obey God's commandments. This is the reason the apostle John could say:

And his commandments are not burdensome,
for everyone born of God overcomes the world.
1 John 5:3b-4a

Once God's commandments are written in our hearts and on our minds, they become a tool to help us conform to the image of Christ. And just what would that look like?

But just as he who called you is holy, so be holy in all you do;
for it is written: "Be holy, because I am holy."
1 Peter 1:15–16

Delight brings us to the understanding that the fulfillment of the Ten Commandments is found not in rituals or religion but in a *relationship* with Jesus as the foundation for our lives. Be ready to see God's commandments from a fresh perspective. God's command to have no other gods before him will melt our hearts as we learn God is jealously and passionately in love with us. Delving into the beauty of God's name will cause us to appreciate the power and the potential contained within his excellent name. Here is a sampling of the principles we'll learn in *Delight*:

- There is life after adultery.
- Sabbath rest is the result of relying on God to meet our needs.

- It takes humility to honor our parents.
- The more intimately we know God, the richer we feel, and
- God mercifully remembers that he made us from dust.

But, most important, we'll come to understand that God's highest purpose in giving us the Ten Commandments is to lead us to Christ and give us new hearts: hearts that *delight* in the laws of God.

* * * * *

All quotations from Scripture come from the *New International Version Study Bible*, Red Letter Edition, edited by Kenneth Barker (Grand Rapids, MI: Zondervan Bible Publishers, 1973, 1978, 1984), unless otherwise indicated by abbreviations in parentheses after the source citation. Commonly quoted versions are New King James Version (NKJV), King James Version (KJV), and New Living Translation (NLT).

* * * * *

Please consider having a journal available to document your thoughts, particularly as they relate to the end-of-chapter discussion questions.

Table of Contents

INTRODUCTION

Ten days prior to my father's death we had our last conversation. Daddy was fully Daddy that day. He'd recently had his car inspected, visited my stepmother at her nursing home, been to Kroger's, and attended to his Amway coffee account.

A few days after that conversation, Paul J. Hinton died of congestive heart failure. I recall our last conversation, during which Daddy gave specific advice, instructions he wanted me to consider following. As this was our last conversation, his request was now all the more significant to me, not only because it was our last conversation, but because this conversation succinctly expressed the heart of my father. If I'd never known Daddy for nearly fifty-seven years, his last words would have been enough to express the totality of his heart and character. They were full of mercy, love, generosity and good will.

Last words stay with you. Last words linger in your ears. Last words are oftentimes marching orders for how to carry on without the one you love.

Before ascending to Heaven, Jesus didn't focus on his life's accomplishments—healing the sick, raising the dead, walking on water. His words focused on what was most important to him.

> *"Teach these new disciples to obey all the commands I have given you. And be sure of this: I am with you always, even to the end of the age."*
> Matthew 28:19 (NLT)

Teach them to obey all my commands: herein lies the heart of Jesus' last words.

- I've given you wonderful things in my law.
- When you walk, they will guide you.
- When you sleep, they will watch over you.
- When you awake, they will speak to you.

- My commands are a lamp and a light for teaching.
- They will correct you.
- In them you will find great peace, and nothing can make you stumble.
(Psalm 119:18, 165; Proverbs 6:22–23)

O, how God wants us to know him—to delight in him! God loves us, and his commandments are an expression of that love. They are wonderful, stable and strong and full of wisdom. *They watch over us.* How can this be anything but love?

It can be difficult to receive instructions from someone who doesn't know you, doesn't love you. Our first inclination is to question that person's motives, especially if the instructions require that we take a different life course. Not so with God. His motivation *is* love. His commandments are an expression of that love, to keep us protected, out of danger and positioned for a life he can bless.

I'm reminded of when our son, Aaron, was about three years old. We lived on a busy street in Madisonville, KY. Money was tight. Yet his daddy and I spent the totality of our tax refund that year to put a chain link fence around our back yard. We wanted Aaron to be free to play and enjoy his sandbox and water hose. But in order for him to play, he had to be protected from harm. I remember Aaron examining the fence the first day it was installed. He went straight to the gate. He pushed, pulled and tugged at it. He thought he wanted out.

But soon Aaron started having fun in his yard. He could bring toys outside, have birthday parties with cousins and neighborhood friends, play on his new swing set, even stand close to the street without fear of being hit by a car. He was safe exploring new territory, and in no time at all Aaron didn't even notice he was playing inside a fence. He was having too much fun!

DELIGHT

I praise you because I am fearfully and wonderfully made . . .

Psalm 139:14a

Chapter 1

The Foundation

"God Thinks You're Wonderful."

In this chapter you will . . .

- discover why it's important to believe God has a destiny for your life;
- understand how your spirit is strengthened;
- identify personal hindrances to spending time alone with God.

Hebrew/Greek word studies: friend, table, ordained, fearfully, wonderfully, secret, deceitful, wicked, delight

The foundation for our faith begins with the understanding that in order for God to have fellowship with us, he created us *in his image*. God is relational. God loves it when we spend time with him. He is the ultimate friend who believes in us, will stick by us, and will always tell us the truth. God wants to be our closest friend, guiding us throughout our lives and providing us with strength to reach our God-ordained destiny.

Indeed, we are fearfully and wonderfully made. God created us in order that we live out a specific, ordained life. He has set us apart, formed, framed and squeezed us into the person we are. God has gifted us with specific talents and abilities that will enable us to fulfill the life he has planned for us. It's true that God has ordained our days and our futures, even before we were born! (Psalm 139:14–16).

In order to understand the love God has for us (and the plans he has for our lives), we must take time to be still and hear his voice. Some specific benefits to meditating upon the laws of God are that sin is described and defined, and the consequences of sin are clearly revealed. God's laws were given to help guide and watch over us, to speak to us and act as a lamp to lead us in the way of life. Hear the passion of the psalmist, David, for the laws of God: "Your hands made me and fashioned me; give me understanding that I may learn your commands." (Psalm 119:73). And David's son, Solomon (believed to be the wisest man who ever lived), held the same esteem for the laws of God: "My son, do not forget my teaching, but keep my commands in your heart, for they will prolong your life many years and bring you prosperity" (Proverbs 3:1-2).

Question: What is a friend? How would you define a friend? We've all had friends come and go in our lives, friends who are sometimes given to us for a season, gifts from God enriching our lives and leaving us with the fondest of memories. We've also had friends who inflicted much sorrow, betrayal, and dishonesty. They too have enriched our lives by causing us to lean in to Jesus to help understand the purpose of the pain.

A friend is "a person attached to another by feelings of affection or personal regard. A person who is on good terms with another, not hostile, kind, supportive, inclined to approve, amicable" (*Random House Dictionary*, 530). In short, a friend is a person you like being around and who likes being with you.

A man who has friends must himself be friendly.
But there is a friend who sticks closer than a brother.
Faithful are the wounds of a friend.
Proverbs 18:24, Proverbs 27:6a (NKJV)

Friend: Hebrew, *ahab* (aw-hab'): (from a root meaning "to have affection for, to be loved ") friend, beloved
Here we see just a few attributes of a true friend: he is friendly toward you, sticks closer to you than a brother, and is so devoted that even the wounds he inflicts can be trusted.

Are you ready to get to know God as this kind of friend? For this to happen, you will have to listen carefully as he speaks to you through his Word. Remember that best friends often like to whisper their secrets, so expect a soft voice, and be ready to lean in to hear what God has to say. Stay there a while. Ponder God's voice until you can articulate what he's saying to you.

PREPARING TO MEET WITH GOD

You prepare a table before me in the presence of my enemies.
You anoint my head with oil; my cup overflows.
Surely goodness and mercy shall follow me all the days of my life,
and I will dwell in the house of the Lord forever.
Psalms 23:5-6

Table: Hebrew, *shulchan* (shool-khawn′): a table, as in a spread-out meal-table.

You've heard the phrase: "Wow! That was quite a spread!" But have you ever had someone set a table and spread it full of food just for you–just you? Imagine how that would make you feel. Now imagine your hostess anointing your head with oil, expressing deep affection for you, and giving focused, undivided attention to you–only you.

"Anointing was an ancient custom practiced by the Egyptians and afterward by the Greeks and Romans and other nations. Olive oil was used, either pure or mixed with fragrant and costly spices, often brought from a long distance (Matt 26:7). Anointing was done not only as a part of a ceremony in connection with the coronation of kings (2 Kings 11:12) and at the installation of the High Priest (Psalm 133:2), *but also as an act of courtesy and hospitality toward a guest* " (Freeman, 313; italics mine).

Then Jesus six days before the passover
came to Bethany, where Lazarus was, which had been dead,
whom he raised from the dead.
There they made him a supper; and Martha served:
but Lazarus was one of them who sat at the table with him.
Then took Mary a pound of ointment of spikenard, very costly,
and anointed the feet of Jesus, and wiped his feet with her hair:
and the house was filled with the odor of the ointment.
John 12:1-3 (KJV)

As an act of hospitality toward the Lord *and* as a gift to yourself, I'd like you to consider preparing a table where you and God can meet together. Make it a special place, a setting which reflects your personality. Have fun with this idea. Be creative, even a little silly if you want. Slip away and enjoy setting a table for your Guest.

My setting is in an upstairs room over our garage. I inherited a chair that belonged to my daddy over fifty years ago, and that's where I go to meet with my heavenly Father. I have pictures of my husband, my two sons, and my grandmother wearing her apron, washing dishes at her kitchen sink. I'm surrounded by candles, pretty vases, some favorite books, my academic diplomas and a treadmill I ignore much too often.

Treadmill aside, this room has a calming effect on me. It has a "come hither to" atmosphere to it. Good things happen at my table—eternal, life-changing things.

King of Hearts

by Pat Menser

If I could but steal a few moments with you.
Stop. And take time for a "How do you do?"
Acknowledge the presence of Most Sovereign King,
Master, Creator of all this earth brings.

I'd bow in your honor and most humbly ask
That you'd open your heart, and make known my task.
I'd ask *not* that my will, but that yours be said.
That your every desire would be spoken and read

On my heart, in my mind, and then quickly obeyed,
Without hesitation, no thought of delay.
For this is the process, this is the start
Of crowning you daily the *King of my heart.*

But when you pray, go into your room,
close the door and pray to your Father, who is unseen.
Then your Father, who sees what is done in secret, will reward you.
Matthew 6:6

GOD, OUR CREATOR

So God created man in his own image,
in the image of God he created him;
male and female he created them.
Genesis 1:27

God created you in the image of himself. He describes this creative process in Psalm 139:14a:

I praise you because I am fearfully and wonderfully made . . .

What exactly did David have in mind when he used the words "fearfully" and "wonderfully"? The Holy Spirit had every style of language, every word, every nuance of speech at his disposal to describe the conception and creation of life. Yet, the Spirit of God led David to pen two specific words to convey a very special message.

Fearfully: Hebrew, *yare* (yaw-ray'): to be frightened to the point of reverence.

This is the same word David used when he said:

You alone are to be feared.
In the council of the holy ones God is greatly feared;
he is more awesome than all who surround him.
For great is the Lord and most worthy of praise;
he is to be feared above all gods.
Psalms 76:7a, 89:7, 96:4 (emphases mine)

The creation of life is a phenomenon that is revered to the point of actually fearing God. Imagine, if you will, the "aura of reverence" surrounding God as he created you.

The second word used to describe the creation of life was "wonderfully," and David wasn't exaggerating this point one bit.

Wonderfully: Hebrew, *palah* (paw-law'): to distinguish, to set apart, to make a difference, to be separate, to make wonderfully

I praise you because I am fearfully and wonderfully made;
your works are wonderful, I know that full well.
Psalm 139:14

Can you feel David's confidence as he writes these words? David knows "full well" that he's a child of God created in the image of God. David understands his divine heritage and his godly ancestry.

There are those who would like us to forget that fact. They don't want us to know our divine heritage. They want us ignorant of the truth that, just like David, we share in the divine distinction of being "fearfully" and "wonderfully" made in the image of God himself. And just where exactly does God create such masterpieces?

My frame was not hidden from you when I was made in the secret place.
When I was woven together in the depths of the earth,
your eyes saw my unformed body.
Psalm 139:15

Secret/depths of the earth: Hebrew, *cether* (say'-ther): cover, hiding place, place of protection

Inside a hidden, covered place of protection, God used great skill to fabricate, variegate in color and then to embroider every detail about you. No wonder he knows the very hairs on your head. The size, texture, and color were all chosen by him.

Years ago I crocheted a lovely afghan. It's made with soft, mint-green yarn, and has a pattern of white flowing through it, a scalloped seashell border and it's . . . it's . . . well, it's beautiful. Loving my afghan and thinking highly of its craftsmanship is easy for me to do. After all, I put so much of me, my time, my work, *myself* into its creation.

But before I crocheted the first stitch of my afghan, before the color or type of yarn was decided upon, before I made my trip to Wal-Mart to purchase the yarn, I took inventory of my home in order to determine the kind of afghan that would best complement my surroundings. The intention of my afghan was that it be a part of our family for years, perhaps generations. Therefore, much thought went into the selection of color, size, design and pattern, and I'm immovable in my conviction that God created you with the same careful planning. The point is this: How does God's affection for his creation compare to my affection for a mint green afghan?

All the days ordained for me
were written in your book before one of them came to be.
Psalm 139:16

Ordained/fashioned: Hebrew, *yatsar* (yaw-tsar'): determined, formed, framed; to make or purpose, to squeeze into shape

When I look at the word "ordained," I'm drawn to the sequence of its definition. God determined the lives we would have, he formed and framed us in a way that would enable us to fulfill his purposes for our lives, and then squeezed us into shape. This "squeezing into shape" is a life-long process termed "sanctification": being conformed to the image of Christ.

BE STILL AND HEAR

For we are God's workmanship,
created in Christ Jesus to do good works,
which God prepared in advance for us to do.
When I was woven together in the depths of the earth,
your eyes saw my unformed body.
All the days ordained for me
were written in your book before one of them came to be.
Ephesians 2:10, Psalm 139:15b–16

It's hard to grasp the concept that God knows the steps we'll take before we take them and the paths we'll choose before we choose them. That being the case, it only stands to reason that God knows the mistakes we'll make before we make them. And he loves us anyway.

The fact that God knows the path our lives *should* take doesn't mean he'll force us to follow that path. God set this precedent in the Garden of Eden when he clearly expressed his will to Adam and Eve and then left the choice to obey or disobey to them. God has promised, however, that if we choose to seek him, we will find him.

Here I am! I stand at the door and knock.
If anyone hears My voice and opens the door,
I will come in to him and eat with him, and he with me.
I love those who love me, and those who seek me find me.
Revelation 3:20, Proverbs 8:17

But Satan has strategically placed landmines in our life, detours along our ordained pathway.

And no wonder, for Satan himself masquerades as an angel of light.
The heart is deceitful above all things,
and desperately wicked;
who can know it?
2 Corinthians 11:14, Jeremiah 17:9 (KJV)

Deceitful: Hebrew, *aqob* (aw-kobe'): swollen up, fraudulent, crooked, deceitful, polluted
Wicked: Hebrew, *anash* (aw-nash'): frail, feeble, incurable, sick

There is a way that seems right to a man,
but in the end it leads to death.
Proverbs 16:25

The point is: there are "other voices" trying to mimic the voice of God. So how can we be sure we're hearing God's voice when everyone is speaking at the same time? One way is to mirror the words we're hearing against God's words spoken in the Ten Commandments. We can be sure God will never ask us to break one of his commands in order to follow his voice and find his will for our life.

The psalms are filled with pleas from King David, asking to hear the voice of God. Yes, David understood he was created in the image of God. That he was clear about. But maybe more important: David knew what he didn't know.

Your hands have made me and fashioned me;
give me understanding, that I may learn Your commandments.
Psalm 119:73 (NKJV)

A SINFUL SILHOUETTE

You are created in the image of God.
You are fearfully and wonderfully made.
God made specific decisions pertaining to every aspect of your creation.
God enjoyed creating you.
But you were not created perfect.
You were born with a curse upon your life.
I know it's a dreadful pill to swallow–
but sometimes the truth is bittersweet.

Surely I was sinful at birth, sinful from the time my mother conceived me.
Psalm 51:5

Sinful while still in our mothers' wombs? Sinful from the moment we were conceived? How could this be? We can thank our ancestors, Adam and Eve, for this predicament; for just as the first watermelon carried within it the seed for all future watermelons, so did Adam carry within him the seed for all mankind. We were in him. *You* were in him, right there with Adam when he chose to sin against God in the Garden of Eden.

Therefore, just as sin entered the world through one man,
and death through sin,
and in this way death came to all men,
because all sinned.
Romans 5:12

And so a conflict rages within us.

For the sinful nature desires what is contrary to the Spirit,
and the Spirit what is contrary to the sinful nature.
They are in conflict with each other,
so that you do not do what you want.
I know that nothing good lives in me, that is, in my sinful nature.
For I have the desire to do what is good, but I cannot carry it out. . .
So I find this law at work:
When I want to do good,
evil is right there with me.
Galatians 5:17, Romans 7:18–21

Now here's the scripture I've been working toward:

For in my inner being I delight in God's law.
Romans 7:22

Delight: Greek, *sunedomai* (soo-nay'dom-ahee): to rejoice in with oneself, to feel satisfaction

What I'm about to write is a critical point as we move forward in the study of God's commandments. Paul writes that he "delights in God's law" *as a follower of Christ* (Acts, Chapter 9). Paul has had a supernatural change of heart. He's gone from breathing out murderous threats against the Lord's disciples (Acts 9:1) to realizing he is God's chosen instrument to carry Jesus' name to the Gentiles and their kings, and before the people of Israel (Acts 9:15). The following scriptures help explain the transformation of Paul's heart.

I will give you a new heart and put a new spirit in you;
I will remove from you your heart of stone and give you a heart of flesh.
And I will put my Spirit in you and move you to follow my decrees
and be careful to keep my laws.
The Lord your God will circumcise your hearts and the hearts of your descendants,
so that you may love him with all your heart and with all your soul, and live.
"This is the covenant I will make with them after that time, says the Lord.
I will put my laws in their hearts, and I will write them on their minds."
Ezekiel 36:26–27, Deuteronomy 30:6, Hebrews 10:16

So now we have the context for who Paul is. He's a man with a heart that has the laws of God written on it: laws that were once external and as hard as stone are now internal, engraved into a heart of flesh.

The next question that needs answering is: To whom is Paul writing when he speaks of his inner being delighting in the laws of God?

To all in Rome who are loved by God and called to be saints:
Grace and peace to you from God our Father and from the Lord Jesus Christ.
First, I thank my God through Jesus Christ for all of you,
because your faith is being reported all over the world.
For in my inner being I delight in God's law.
Romans 1:7–8, Romans 7:22 (emphasis mine)

Paul is speaking to fellow saints living in Rome, men and women whose faith is being reported all over the world. As with Paul, God's laws are written on their hearts as well. So Paul's audience is Romans with changed hearts, as opposed to Romans whose hearts have yet to be changed.

We each fall into one of those categories:
- Romans with changed hearts,
- Romans without changed hearts.

Please keep these two very different audiences in mind as you move forward in studying God's commandments. If you're a person with a changed heart, an in-depth study of these commandments will be an absolute delight to you as they help you become more like your Father.

"Be holy, because I am holy."
1 Peter 1:16

And if you're a person who has yet to put your faith in Christ, these same commandments will help guide you to do just that.

Before this faith came,
we were held prisoners by the law, locked up until faith should be revealed.
So the law was put in charge to lead us to Christ
that we might be justified by faith.
Galatians 3:23–24

FEED ME, PLEASE

Almost four months ago God blessed our family with a second granddaughter, Julia Hinton Menser. Big blue eyes, dark hair. I affectionately call her Baby Doll. Let me tell you something about Baby Doll: she lets you know when she's hungry. She expects her bottle to be warm and ready to go the moment she feels that first hunger pang. She feels. *We hear.* We obey!

Our souls are much more subtle. But don't mistake the quiet as lack of hunger.

My soul is weary with sorrow;
strengthen me according to your word.
Psalm 119:28

I've been there before: times when I'm drained, emotionally empty, spiritually dry. Friends and family would try to comfort me, offering their support, bringing food, doing their best—but my deepest source of relief always came through Scripture. I remember when I had full knee replacement surgery. One dear friend brought me a feast of food along with a print-out of scriptures related to having strong knees and renewed strength. I taped that piece of paper to the side of my nightstand, and as I lay flat on my back, I had only to turn my head to be encouraged by the word of God.

Taste and see that the Lord is good;
blessed is the man who takes refuge in him.
How sweet are your words to my taste,
sweeter than honey to my mouth!
Psalm 34:8, 119:103

Foundation

PRINCIPLES

1. We are fearfully and wonderfully made, *masterpieces* created by God himself!

2. Our days were determined before we were even born.

3. Spending time with God develops, deepens and strengthens our friendship with him.

4. God's will for our lives will never contradict or require us to break his commandments.

5. The fact that God knows the path our lives should take does not mean he will constrain us to follow that path.

6. God's commandments clarify what sin is, thus leading us to Christ to save us from our sin.

7. We were born with the sin nature of Adam.

8. Our spirit hungers for spiritual food.

9. We can strengthen our spirit by feeding our eyes and ears the Word of God.

10. We can be deceived by the desires of our hearts.

11. God wants to be our closest friend, guiding us throughout our lives and through specific conflicts, providing spiritual strength for us to reach our God-ordained destiny.

Foundation

DISCUSSION QUESTIONS

1. Did you set a table for Jesus and yourself? What were some of the personal items you used to decorate this special place?

2. After studying the definition of a true friend, take a minute to write the names of the true friends in your life.

3. Reflect on the words "fearfully" and "wonderfully" as written in Psalm 139:14–16. How can these words enrich your life?

4. How do you feel about the way God created you?

5. Revelation 3:20 says, "Behold, I stand at the door and knock. If anyone hears My voice and opens the door, I will come in to him and dine with him, and he with me." Try to draw a mental picture of how this verse would look.

6. Is there a hindrance in your life that consistently prevents you from spending time alone with God? Does something or someone come to mind?

7. Is it within your power to remove this hindrance? Answer yes or no.

8. If you answered yes, what specific action must you take to remove this hindrance?

9. Think about what it takes for you to "learn" something. What are some of the conditions that need to be in place for you to be able to learn?

10. Matthew 6:22–23a explains how spiritual food enters your spirit:

The eye is the lamp of the body.
If your eyes are good, your whole body will be full of light.
But if your eyes are bad, your whole body will be full of darkness.

Rewrite these verses in a way that is practical for you and can apply to your everyday life.

11. "Your hands have made me and fashioned me; give me understanding, that I may learn Your commandments" (Psalm 119:73.) These words reflect how David felt about God's commandments. If they reflect your heart, write out some of the reasons you want to have a better understanding of God's commandments.

For I, the Lord your God, am a jealous God.

Exodus 20:5a

Chapter 2

Have No Other Gods Before Me

Exodus 20:3

"God Wants All of You."

In this chapter you will . . .

- read examples of Pharaoh's tactics to keep God's children in bondage;
- understand God's attitude toward people living in bondage;
- appreciate the meaning of God being "jealous" over you;
- see how parental examples of having, or not having, other gods in our lives has a direct impact upon the lives of our children.

Hebrew/Greek word studies: gods, carved/graven, know, mixed, jealous, visiting, iniquity, mercy, glory

In this chapter we learn that God is passionately in love with his children. God's desire is that we pursue his love and worship him wholeheartedly. Satan, on the other hand, wants to keep God's people in bondage and unable to freely worship God.

Before we came to our new life in Christ, we could be compared to the Hebrew child imprisoned in Egypt. We were in spiritual chains, slaves to our flesh, distanced from our rightful inheritance, and living under the dictatorship of a grueling taskmaster. God saw our suffering and he knew our need for spiritual freedom. It was then, when God combined a Father's compassion with the blood of his Son, that he secured our pathway to spiritual freedom.

As we journey forward in this freedom, we learn that God is good and that he wants to provide for us. We'll come to understand that God does what he says he'll do—and that God rewards not only those who build their lives upon his commands, *but their children as well.*

But from everlasting to everlasting the Lord's love is with those who fear him,
and his righteousness with their children's children–
with those who keep his covenant, and remember to obey his precepts.
Psalm 103:17-18

I AM JEALOUS

"You shall have no other gods before Me.
You shall not make for yourself a carved image–
any likeness of anything that is in heaven above, or that is in the earth beneath,
or that is in the water under the earth; you shall not bow down to them nor serve them.
For I, the Lord your God, am a jealous God,
visiting the iniquity of the fathers upon the children to the third and fourth generations
of those who hate Me, but showing mercy to thousands,
to those who love Me and keep My commandments."
Exodus 20:3-6 (NKJV; emphasis mine)

An important component of these two commandments is the phrase: *for I, the Lord your God, am a jealous God.* God is very clear concerning his jealous nature. He makes no apologies for being jealous. We are his. *You* are his. God purchased you, paid for you with the blood of his Son, giving God every right to be possessive in his love for you.

God blessed my husband and me with two sons, Aaron and John. As I study this commandment, a sense of passion and jealousy arises within me as I think about how I would feel toward you (anybody for that matter) if I asked one of my sons to die on your behalf. I would own you; at least that's the way I would feel. I would want you to love me with all your heart, soul, body and mind. You could not appreciate enough the sacrifice I asked my son to make so that I could have eternal life with you. I would want an intimate, committed, passionate relationship with you, and it would sadden me beyond words if you didn't feel the same way toward me.

THE DEVIL WE KNOW

The people of our generation aren't much different from the people of Moses' generation who were imprisoned in Egypt but later set free in order to seek their Promised Land. We, not unlike them, are many times "bent homeward," especially when circumstances become a little rough and we're having difficulty finding our way. We look for the familiar, a sort of "the devil we know is better than the one we don't" kind of mentality.

Our inclination to look backward on our road to freedom comes as no surprise to God. God knows full well our tendency to begin things his way and make our promises and pledges—only to fall back into old patterns, habits and lifestyles.

When Pharaoh let the people go, God did not lead them on the road through the Philistine country, though that was shorter. For God said,
"If they face war, they might change their minds and return to Egypt."
So God led the people around by the desert road toward the Red Sea.
The Israelites went up out of Egypt armed for battle.
Exodus 13:17–18

Interesting. The road to the Israelites' Promised Land was purposefully long and winding. God knew that as soon as the Israelites encountered a war, they would change their minds about their journey to freedom and cow-tail it back to Egypt. Sometimes it's easier to live in bondage than fight the wars which lead us to a land flowing with milk and honey.

Egypt represented a world of endless servitude to an insatiable taskmaster. God wanted to distance his children from Egypt and their familiar lifestyle of bondage and slavery. In freeing his children from Pharaoh's oppression, God left only one reason for them to ever look back at Egypt: gratitude for their freedom.

And God said, "This is how you are to eat it: with your cloak tucked into your belt, your sandals on your feet and your staff in your hand. Eat it in haste; it is the Lord's Passover" (Exodus 12:11). God instituted the yearly Feast of the Passover in order to remind the Hebrews of their exodus from

Egypt—their release from slavery. The unleavened bread was to remind them of their hasty departure (the dough didn't have time to rise). The bitter herbs were reminders of their bitter lives under Pharaoh's rule. Yes, God wanted his children to remember Egypt, but *he never intended for them to desire the predictable life of captivity over the exciting life of faith.*

All of this helps us understand the humanity of the Hebrews and why God found it necessary to nudge their memories before entering their Promised Land. They were about to embark upon the adventure of a lifetime, a journey which included building new lives for themselves in an unfamiliar land. And if they weren't careful, fear of the future and forgetfulness of their bitter past could be their downfall. And so, after distancing his children from Egypt and just before giving his people the Ten Commandments, God chose to remind them of their former bondage.

I am the Lord your God,
who brought you out of the land of Egypt,
out of the house of bondage.
Exodus 20:2 (NKJV)

Again, this was the statement God made to the Hebrew people as they were preparing to follow him into their Promised Land.

ARE YOU FREE?

I'm not asking if you want to be free. I'm not asking if you think you're free. I'm asking, "*Are you free to pursue your Promised Land?*" Please don't answer that question too quickly. You should remember that for years the Hebrews wanted to be released from Egypt in order to worship their God. Wanting to be free and actually being free are not the same thing.

Let's recall that the Hebrew children ached for their freedom. But Pharaoh, just as earnestly, determined to keep the Hebrew race under his control. Blood, frogs, gnats, flies, boils, hail, locust, darkness—none of these plagues were able to convince Pharaoh to relinquish ownership of his Hebrew slaves.

Pharaoh found the God of Moses to be a formidable opponent. Upon realizing this, Pharaoh very cunningly tried to bargain with Moses. If Pharaoh could keep even partial control of his slaves, that was good enough for him. His conciliatory offer to Moses went something like this:

- Go ahead and sacrifice to God, but do it here in Egypt (Exodus 8:25).
- Go to the desert, not very far from Egypt (Exodus 8:28).
- Go, but leave your women and children here in Egypt (Exodus 10:10).
- Go, take your women and children, but leave your livestock (livelihood, business, wealth) here in Egypt (Exodus 10:25).

But Moses refused to negotiate with the devil. Instead, Moses demanded that every trace of the Hebrew race must leave Egypt . . . down to the very last hoof!

Our livestock too must go with us;
not a hoof is to be left behind.
Exodus 10:26b (emphasis mine)

Moses was serious about his pursuit of freedom, and he knew such freedom could only be realized by making a *complete* break from Egypt. "Not a hoof is to be left behind." Satan will hold on to any part of our lives we'll give him. He desperately wants us to remain attached to Egypt, if not wholeheartedly, then at least partially so. If we're serious about following God and his destiny for our lives, then we must be as determined as Moses to make a clean and total break from Egypt, leaving nothing behind . . . not even a hoof.

MOVING FORWARD

Then Moses summoned all the elders of Israel and said to them,
"Go at once and select the animals for your families and slaughter the Passover lamb.
Take a bunch of hyssop, dip it into the blood in the basin
and put some of the blood on the top and on both sides of the doorframe.
Not one of you shall go out the door of his house until morning.
When the Lord goes through the land to strike down the Egyptians,
he will see the blood on the top and sides of the doorframe
and will pass over the doorway,

and he will not permit the destroyer to enter your houses and strike you down.
Exodus 12:21–23 (emphasis mine)

What had to happen before the Hebrews could be free from Pharaoh?
Bloodshed.
What was to be placed on the doorposts of the house of each Hebrew?
The blood of a lamb.
Who were not struck down by the Lord?
Those living in homes covered by blood.
Who were struck down by the Lord?
Those living in homes not covered by blood.

It's always been about blood. In Old Testament days, the blood of a Passover lamb secured freedom for the children of God. Today, in New Testament times, it's the blood of a Passover Lamb (Jesus) that secures our freedom. The shedding of his blood and the acceptance of it over the doorposts of our lives is the way we're set free to leave our past and move forward to fully worship God.

Please notice that God didn't require more bricks, more effort, or more sweat from his children before he set them free. God's gift of freedom was just that—a free gift. Neither did God wait for the Hebrews to become good enough or holy enough in order to earn the right to be set free. God didn't wait for that to happen because he knew it never could happen. There is nothing they could ever do that would merit them the right to freedom. Instead, it was the combination of compassion (flowing from the heart of a loving God: "I have heard their cry. . . I know their sorrows") and blood (flowing from the flesh of a lamb) that paved their way to freedom.

The Lord said, "I have indeed seen the misery of my people in Egypt.
I have heard them crying out because of their slave drivers,
and I am concerned about their suffering.
So I have come down to rescue them from the hand of the Egyptians
and to bring them up out of that land into a good and spacious land,
a land flowing with milk and honey. . ."
Exodus 3:7–8a

Let's not miss the affection and deep connection God feels toward his people.

I see their misery.
I hear them crying.
I am concerned about their suffering.

Know (KJV), Concerned (NIV): Hebrew, *yada* (yaw-dah'): to ascertain, to know by seeing, to observe, to care, to recognize

"To know by observing and reflecting (thinking), and to know by experiencing. It is firsthand knowing and is synonymous with 'hear,' 'see,' and 'perceive.' In addition to the essentially cognitive knowing already presented, this verb has a purely experiential side. The 'knower' has actual involvement with or in the object of the knowing" (Vine, 130).

So I have come down to rescue them from the hand of the Egyptians. . .
Exodus 38:8

Oh, yes. The Knower rescued the Hebrews from the hand of the Egyptians. But that wasn't the only time he would come down to rescue his people. God came down from heaven again, in the flesh of his son Jesus, to rescue us from our enemy and to lead us to a land flowing with milk and honey.

The Word became flesh and made his dwelling among us.
John 1:14a

So remember, wherever you've been and whatever you're going through, God knows your misery, he's seen you crying, he's concerned about your suffering, and he's experiencing it with you.

I'm reminded of a time when my older son, Aaron was about three years old. I'd been sick for several days and was feeling so bad. I tried to keep up our normal routine but soon discovered that even a toddler can tell when Mama's not well. I smile now when I remember lying on the couch, feverish, drained, and in walks Aaron carrying his prized possession, "Mama, you want my 'Dallas-Cowboy-Football-Helmet-Jersey-Shirt'?" (Yes, that's how he referred to it.)

Bless his little cotton-top head—he loved me so much. It hurt him to see his mama sick and suffering, so much so that he was willing to give me his very best if it would make me feel better.

Be sure that God is just as aware of your suffering. Whatever it is that's holding you down, putting you on the couch and preventing you from moving forward toward your Promised Land, God sees the pain it's producing in your life, and he's concerned enough that he was willing to give his very best to make you better.

THE MIXED MULTITUDE

It appears there were "other" people journeying along with the Hebrews as they left Egypt to seek their Promised Land.

And a mixed multitude went up with them also;
and flocks, and herds—a great deal of livestock.
Exodus 12:38 (NKJV; emphasis mine)

Who were the people in this "mixed multitude"? Might they have been Egyptians who had witnessed the power of God in the lives of the Hebrew slaves? Could such power have persuaded these Egyptians to join themselves with the Hebrews as they left Egypt to worship the God of such miracles? Another thought is that the Hebrew race itself was of a mixed multitude. Perhaps there were those whose hearts had not been truly consecrated to the Lord. Maybe they were "tabernacle attendees," rubbing shoulders with Moses and Aaron, participating in all the religious rituals, viewing God as procedure and tradition, but people who weren't following Jehovah with a truly consecrated heart.

Now the mixed multitude who were among them yielded to intense craving;
so the children of Israel also wept again and said:
"Who will give us meat to eat?
We remember the fish which we ate freely in Egypt,
the cucumbers, the melons, the leeks, the onions, and the garlic;
but now our whole being is dried up;
there is nothing at all except this manna before our eyes!"
Numbers 11:4–6b (NKJV)

Mixed: Hebrew, *'ereb* (eh'-reb): a mixture or mongrel race; mingled, mixed people.

Has there *ever* been a group of believers of which all members were pure of heart? Not in Moses' day and certainly not in ours. In a strange sort of way, there's a certain comfort in the knowledge that God allowed people who would eventually fall to lusting to be a part of the exodus of the Hebrew people. Such knowledge should *give us patience* to deal with people today sitting in our church pews, playing on our ball teams, and participating in our youth groups whose lifestyles do not reflect that of a true believer. May we lead them away from their sin and toward God rather than the other way around.

THE FREE GIFT

A person without Christ can be compared to the Hebrew child imprisoned in Egypt–free to leave his chains but choosing to stay behind, distanced from his rightful inheritance, and living his life under the dictatorship of a taskmaster. This imprisoned person has either not been told, or he's heard and refused to believe that the blood of the New Testament Lamb has purchased his freedom. Whatever the reason, this person hasn't received his gift of liberty. How sad that anyone would grow comfortable wearing chains in Egypt when God has provided him a land flowing with milk and honey.

But that's how we think: we've known nothing else except the life of slavery. And what do slaves do? They work. That's what they know, and to ask them to do otherwise is foreign to them.

"Work, work, work, work, work, work, work." That's the message Satan tells us even today. "You can't leave Egypt. You're a slave. These are your roots. This is who you are. It was good enough for your parents and grandparents and it's good enough for you. And if you're even thinking about leaving Egypt, you'll most certainly have to *work yourself out*."

And many of us believe his lies. Thus, we gather our meager utensils of "good works" and, in vain, begin to slowly and methodically work our way toward freedom. It's a grueling, laborious, never-ending, life-long task.

Understand that if we, or the imprisoned Hebrews, thought God's favor could somehow be earned and deserved, the tendency to boast about reaching such an awesome goal would be a powerful temptation. "Look how long and hard I've worked. Aren't I the most disciplined, dedicated, deserving person for freedom that you know? By the way, the only reason you're not free is that you're not willing to work as hard as I work."

There's no question about it. God wants us to depend wholly on him for our exodus from sin into our land of plenty. And you can mark this down: Heaven will be filled with grateful saints who know they were deserving of hell, yet were spared such a fate *only* because of the blood of Jesus.

THE GIFT OF FAITH

If the Israelites could trust God to deliver them from Pharaoh and his armies, wouldn't you think they'd trust God to deliver them from their thirst and hunger? Such grumbling, such lack of faith in God's watchful care for them surely saddened our Lord. Continually God tested his children in the area of having faith in him—continually they failed.

Then Moses said to them, "No one is to keep any of it until morning."
However, some of them paid no attention to Moses;
they kept part of it until morning,
but it was full of maggots and began to smell. So Moses was angry with them.
Exodus 16:19-20

Moses gave clear instructions. His tone was imperative. "No one was to keep any of it until morning." Yet some of them paid no attention.

Well, I'm paying attention. And I've paraphrased the words of Moses to reflect how they apply to my own life: "Believing God won't provide for me is an indicator of my lack of faith in him. God wants me to trust him to meet all my needs, day in and day out. There is no reason to hoard his provisions or worry that there won't be enough."

But then Moses gives us further instruction:

He said to them, "This is what the Lord commanded:
'Tomorrow is to be a day of rest, a holy Sabbath to the Lord.
So bake what you want to bake and boil what you want to boil.
Save whatever is left and keep it until morning.' "
Exodus 16:23

Don't save manna. Do save manna. Which is it? To answer this question we have to ask a question. After being told not to keep manna until morning, and then being told to save whatever manna is left and keep it until morning, what would it take for the Hebrews to follow through with these instructions?

I know I'm taking you on a winding scriptural journey, but stay with me. First, God says not to save any manna from one day to the next; then he tells them there's one day a week when they can save food for the following day. What is he trying to teach them? It couldn't be about keeping a Sabbath Day, since the commandment to keep the Sabbath hasn't yet been given (that doesn't happen until Exodus, chapter 20).

It appears there's a Sabbath *principle* God wants to weave into their understanding, and he's using manna as his object lesson. Again, remember the context of which we speak: we're in Exodus, Chapter 16, and *the Ten Commandments have not yet been given.* What does it mean then that, while God is talking about manna, he says, "Bear in mind that the Lord has given you the Sabbath"?

And God blessed the seventh day and made it holy,
because on it he <u>rested</u> from all the work of creating he had done.
Genesis 2:3

After six days of creating light, the sky, dry ground, vegetation, day and night, birds and great sea creatures, livestock and wild animals, and finally, man, what did God do after he was finished creating?

Rested: Hebrew, *shabath* (shaw-bath'): to repose, to desist from exertion, to leave, to put away (down), to make to rest

This is what God did. He rested. He rested because all was done. This is where God is pointing when he says in Exodus 16:23, 'Tomorrow is to be a day of rest, a holy *Sabbath* to the Lord." And then again in Exodus 16:29a:

"Bear in mind that the Lord has given you the Sabbath; that is why on the sixth day he gives you bread for two days."

Before the Ten Commandments were ever carved on tablets of stone, God used the principle of the Sabbath to teach his children about faith. The Sabbath is synonymous with faith, with resting in God's work finished on our behalf. It takes faith to believe God created the world in six days and that, when God's task was completed, he rested. The Sabbath declares that God is thorough: God is complete and God has everything under control. God's call to "bear in mind that the Lord has given you the Sabbath" was God's way of reminding the Hebrews that they didn't need to worry about not having manna each day or about drawing maggots on the one day they're told to keep extra manna. If God says *not to* gather extra food, have faith, trust and obey him. If God says *to* gather extra food, have faith, trust and obey him. Have faith in the one true God who rested on the seventh day of creation as evidence that he is the Author and Finisher of your faith. If, when God created the world, anything or any need of man had been lacking, God would not have rested.

And it's *because* God rested that we can rest as we remember the Sabbath, keeping it as a principle of life—a life of faith, rest, repose, desisting from exertion, and, most important, gratitude for an all-providing God.

A JEALOUS GOD COMES TO VISIT

Many of us memorized God's first commandment as:

"You shall have no other gods before Me."
Exodus 20:3

and the second commandment as:

"You shall not make for yourself an idol–
any likeness of anything . . ."
Exodus 20:4

Idols are demonically misleading: illusions appearing to be real. Idols can't bless our lives; carved images have no power to protect or provide for us. These substitutes may provide a temporary measure of comfort, but as false gods attach themselves to our lives, they become blood-sucking taskmasters, driving us deeper and deeper into their clutches. They want to be adored. They want to be idolized. They want our worship and dependence. They are like leeches: drawing life for themselves while draining it from ours. God says his children are not to worship anything he has ever created,

. . . in the form of anything that is in heaven above,
or on the earth beneath or in the waters below.
You shall not bow down to them or worship them;
for I, the Lord your God, am a jealous God. . .
Do not worship any other god,
for the Lord, whose name is Jealous, is a jealous God.
Exodus 20:4b–5a, 34:14

Jealous: Hebrew, *qanna* (kan-naw'): envious, provoked to zealous behavior

Qanna as a verb: "God is not tainted with the negative connotation of the verb. His holiness does not tolerate competitors or those who sin against Him. In no single passage in the whole Old Testament is God described as envious. Even in those texts where the adjective 'jealous' is used, it might be more appropriate to understand it as 'zealous' " (Vine, 124).

Qanna as an adjective: "occurs six times in the Old Testament. The word refers directly to the attributes of God's justice and holiness, as He is the sole object of human worship and does not tolerate man's sin" (Vine, 125).

God is very up-front in describing himself as jealous. Jealous is his name. We need to take note that, as believers, we're in a relationship with a person who is extremely jealous of us. Furthermore, God is clear about the way he handles his jealousy.

You shall have no other gods before me.
You shall not make for yourself an idol in the form of anything. . . .
for I the Lord your God, am a jealous God,
punishing the children for the sin of the fathers
to the third and fourth generation of those who hate me. . .
Exodus 20:3-6

Punishing/ visiting: Hebrew, *paqad* (paw-kad'): to do judgment by any means, to have oversight, to punish, to call to remembrance, to oversee, to deposit, to avenge, to bestow, to deliver

The King James translation of Exodus 20:5b says:

For I, the Lord thy God, am a jealous God,
visiting the iniquity of the fathers upon the children
unto the third and fourth generation of them who hate me. . .

Sin/Iniquity: Hebrew, *avon* (aw-vone'): perversity, evil, mischief

The commandment to "have no other gods" is more serious than many of us may think. God says that, as a father, he will oversee, do judgment by any means, punish and call to remembrance the perversity, evil and mischief of his children unto the third and fourth generations. Do you see the gravity of this commandment, the importance of the choices you make? Even now our choices are having an effect upon our children and descendants. By obeying God's command to "have no other gods before me," we can send iniquity on a detour not only from our lives but also from the lives of our children, grandchildren, and even our great-grandchildren. It's bad enough to endure the consequences of our own sins, but to think that our children could suffer for our sins is a sobering thought, indeed.

We've all had events happen in our lives which caused us to think, "I've done nothing to deserve such hardship." Could it be you're living within the third or fourth generation of a family who "had other gods before him"? Maybe you were in the process of being "visited" with your forefather's iniquity. Now, before you quickly blame someone else for your past or present circumstances, it would be wise to first ask God to search your heart and reveal choices you've made which have contributed to your difficult circumstances.

You have set our iniquities before you,
our secret sins in the light of your presence.
Search me, O God, and know my heart;
test me, and know my anxious thoughts.
See if there be any offensive way in me,
and lead me in the way everlasting.
Psalm 90:8,139:23–24

BENEFITS OF A RIGHTEOUS HERITAGE

The commandment to "have no other gods before me" can appear weighted with negatives and bordering on harshness. At this point you may regret buying this book and be ready to forget about this commandment. Before you do anything drastic, please remember the desire of your spirit!

Your hands have made me and fashioned me;
give me understanding, that I may learn Your commandments.
For in my inner being I delight in God's law.
Psalm 119:73 (NKJV), Romans 7:22

Keep going. You haven't heard the rest of the story. If you'll turn this commandment over, you'll see that its underside is soft, sweet, and deliciously appealing.

Judgment Side:

You shall not make for yourself a carved image–any likeness of anything that is in heaven above, or that is in the earth beneath, or that is in the water under the earth; you shall not bow down to them nor serve them. For I, the Lord your God, am a jealous God, visiting the iniquity of the fathers upon the children to the third and fourth generations of those who hate me,

Mercy Side:

. . . but showing mercy unto thousands of them who love me,
and keep my commandments.
Exodus 20:4-6b (NKJV)

Accentuate this mercy promise with another:
But the mercy of the Lord is from everlasting to everlasting on those who fear Him,
and His righteousness to children's children.
Psalm 103:17-18 (NKJV)

Mercy: Hebrew, *checed* (kheh'-sed): kindness, favor, beauty, pity

Yes, God does say that he will visit the sins of the fathers upon their children, unto the third and fourth generation. *But he also says he will bless those who fear him and their children.* Just as parents enjoy blessing children who obey them, God delights in showing kindness toward those who delight in his commandments. We may have thought the commandment to "have no other gods before me" was too heavy to enjoy, when what we needed to do was look at it from both sides, particularly its "good side." We all have one, you know.

Some of us enjoyed a godly heritage. We lived in a home where God's commandments were embraced by our parents and taught to us as children. Others come from families where God's Word was never served to them. We're empty and longing to know more about the God who created us. We too are blessed. We're blessed because we are hungry. Our parents may not have loved God's commandments; they may have strayed from his Word and suffered the consequences, but we can be grateful even for this, for in their suffering they have shown us the wrong way, the way that will not satisfy our hunger and will not lead to joy. They have shown us the road *not* to travel.

A RICH INHERITANCE

The fear of the Lord is the beginning of wisdom;
a good understanding have all those who do His commandments.
Psalm 111:10a (NKJV)

He decreed statutes for Jacob and established the law in Israel,
which he commanded our forefathers to teach their children,
so the next generation would know them, even the children yet to be born,
and they in turn would tell their children. Then they would put their trust in God
and would not forget his deeds but would keep his commands.
They would not be like their forefathers–a stubborn and rebellious generation,
whose hearts were not loyal to God, whose spirits were not faithful to him.
Psalm 78:5-8

I seek you with all my heart; do not let me stray from your commands.
I have hidden your word in my heart that I might not sin against you.
Psalm 119:10-11

But from everlasting to everlasting the Lord's love is with those who fear him,
and his righteousness with their children's children–
with those who keep his covenant and remember to obey his precepts.
Psalm 103:17-18

The righteous man leads a blameless life;
blessed are his children after him.
Proverbs 20:7

It just gets better and better!

Children's children are the crown of old men,
and the glory of children are their fathers.
Proverbs 17:6 (KJV)

Glory: Hebrew, *tiphereth* (tif-eh'-reth): ornament, beauty, bravery, honor

Let's slow down here a minute. This is important information. When we become parents, we have the awesome opportunity of providing beauty, bravery and honor to our children. How will you do this? By walking in integrity, keeping God's covenant, and remembering his commandments.

No Other gods

PRINCIPLES

1. God is passionately, jealously in love with us.

2. When God created the world, if anything had been lacking or any need of man unfulfilled, God would not have rested.

3. Jesus can deliver us from our bondages.

4. In order to find our destiny in life, we must be willing to let go of the familiar.

5. God's plan for our lives will include exercises in faith.

6. When circumstances become difficult, man's inclination is to return to the familiar.

7. Satan will hold on to any part of our lives we will give him.

8. Idols usurp our energy.

9. We should be aware of relationships that encourage us to lust and crave for the things of the world.

10. Parental choices can affect their children, both positively and negatively, to the third and fourth generations.

11. God judges each man according to his own ways.

12. Satan would have us try to work or earn our salvation. This is an affront to Jesus and the cross.

13. God clearly says in his Word that "You are mine."

No Other gods

DISCUSSION QUESTIONS

1. Describe your life of bondage before the blood of the Lamb set you free.

2. The Hebrews longed for leeks, melons, garlic and onions. List any "fond memories" that try to lure you back to your former way of life.

3. Why do you think Pharaoh was willing to allow the Hebrews to worship God in the desert "not very far from Egypt" (Exodus 8:25)?

4. Why do you think Pharaoh wanted the men to "go" but to leave their women and children in Egypt (Exodus 10:10)?

5. Why do you think Pharaoh wanted the Hebrews to leave their livestock in Egypt (Exodus 10:26)?

6. Is there a part of your life which hasn't been totally given to God? Is there a "hoof" that remains in Egypt? Take this time to identify any area in your life that Satan holds in even partial possession. Name your hoof.

7. How does it make you feel that God "knows" the bondage in your life and it causes him to be concerned for you?

8. Since becoming a Christian, has there been a particular person/mixed multitude whose influence leads you to lust after the things of the world, hindering your walk with God?

9. How does the Sabbath principle relate to having no other gods in your life?

10. Do you think God has feelings?

Lord, our Lord, how excellent is your name in all the earth.

Psalm 8:1a

Chapter 3

Do Not Misuse the Lord's Name

Exodus 20:7

"Friends Build You Up."

In this chapter you will . . .

- appreciate the effects the name of Jesus has upon the world;
- acknowledge body parts created with the ability to praise God's name;
- contrast righteous and perverse speech.

Hebrew/Greek word studies: Immanuel, Jesus, excellent, hallowed, vain, perverse

Honoring God's name is an issue of the heart. People who understand the sacrifice of Jesus, his servant-heart toward us, and his humble and obedient nature will value such qualities and honor his name. Those who have yet to recognize the character of Jesus will be inclined to treat Jesus' name in a common and useless manner. Keep in mind that the command to "not take the Lord's name in vain" was given by a Father who longs to be known by his children.

Jesus was not interested in building a reputation for himself. Jesus' focus was on hearing the voice of his Father and serving the people his Father loved. This chapter highlights the characteristics of the excellent, exalted, *strong* name of a humble man named Jesus.

AN EXALTED NAME

Therefore God exalted him to the highest place
and gave him the name that is above every name,
that at the name of Jesus every knee should bow,
in heaven and on earth and under the earth,
and every tongue confess that Jesus Christ is Lord,
to the glory of God the Father.
Because your love is better than life, my lips will glorify you.
I will praise you as long as I live, and in your name I will lift up my hands.
Let them praise his name with dancing
and make music to him with tambourine and harp.
Philippians 2:9–11, Psalm 63:3–4, 149:3 (emphases mine)

Oh, the power of that name! Our lips, hands, even our feet were created with the ability to praise the name of God. Jesus gave us the best example of how we are to treat the name of his Father:

"This then is how you should pray:
'Our Father in heaven,
hallowed be your name.' "
Matthew 6:9

Name: a word by which a person is known.

Many times we have a preconceived image of what a name represents, based upon our experience of how people with the same name have behaved. There is, however, one name that can be compared to no other.

O Lord, our Lord,
how majestic is your name in all the earth!
Psalm 8:1

I love the exclamation point in this verse. Love it!

Majestic/Excellent: Hebrew, *shem* (shame): a position of honor, authority, character, fame and renown

The Lord's name is excellent, glorious, full of honor, authority, character and fame. Before even the conception of God's son, God sent an angel to declare the name he was to be given.

Therefore the Lord himself will give you a sign:
The virgin will be with child and will give birth to a son,
and will call him Immanuel.
Isaiah 7:14

Immanuel: Hebrew, *Immanuw'el* (Im-maw-noo-ale'): God with us.

This is how the birth of Jesus Christ came about:
His mother Mary was pledged to be married to Joseph,
but before they came together, she was found to be with child through the Holy Spirit.
Because Joseph her husband was a righteous man
and did not want to expose her to public disgrace,
he had in mind to divorce her quietly.
But after he had considered this, an angel of the Lord appeared to him in a dream
and said, "Joseph son of David, do not be afraid to take Mary home as your wife,
because what is conceived in her is from the Holy Spirit.
She will give birth to a son, and you are to give him the name Jesus,
because he will save his people from their sins.
All this took place to fulfill what the Lord had said through the prophet:
"The virgin will be with child and will give birth to a son,
and they will call him Immanuel"–which means, "God with us."
Matthew 1:18–23

God with us. What does God with us look like? Jesus tells us that if we want to see what his Father looks like, then look at Jesus.

"Anyone who has seen me has seen the Father.
How can you say, 'Show us the Father'?
Don't you believe that I am in the Father, and that the Father is in me?"
John 14:9b–10a

So let's look at Jesus–not his face or his body but his character, the essence of who he is.

Your attitude should be the same as that of Christ Jesus;
Who, being in the very nature God,
did not consider equality with God something to be grasped,
but made himself nothing,
taking the very nature of a servant,
being made in human likeness.
And being found in appearance as a man,
he humbled himself and became obedient to death–
even death on a cross!
Philippians 2:5–8

Immanuel, God with us, Jesus, Savior from sin . . .

- took on the very nature of God,
- didn't consider equality with God something to be grasped,
- made himself nothing,
- took on the very nature of a servant,
- was made in human likeness and appeared as a man,
- humbled himself,
- was obedient even unto death.

If you want to see into the heart of God, then look at the character of his Son: like Father, like Son.

Therefore, God also has highly exalted him
and given him the name which is above every name. . .
Philippians 2:9a

Exalted: Greek, *huperupsoo* (hoop-er-oop-so′-o): to elevate above others, to raise to the highest position.

And because the name of Jesus is so highly exalted, what will someday happen at the very mention of his name?

That at the name of Jesus every knee should bow,
in heaven and on earth and under the earth,
and every tongue confess that Jesus Christ is Lord,
to the glory of God the Father.
Philippians 2:10–11

A STRONG NAME

The name of Jesus provides salvation.
Acts 4:12, 10:43

The name of Jesus releases the gift of the Holy Spirit.
Acts 2:38

The name of Jesus provides healing.
Acts 3:6, 16, 4:10

The name of Jesus produces signs and wonders.
Acts 4:30

The name of Jesus may cause men to suffer disgrace.
Acts 5:41

The name of Jesus may cause havoc.
Acts 9:21

The name of Jesus causes men to preach fearlessly.
Acts 9:27

The name of Jesus has been reason for men to risk their lives.
Acts 15:26

The name of Jesus is able to cause spirits to come out of people.
Acts 16:16-18

My friend and prolific songwriter, Ruth Davis, expresses the name of Jesus this way:

"There's healing in the name of Jesus.
There is power in his precious blood.
The chastisement of our peace, placed on him brings release.
Be made well, be made whole, be healed."

Jesus appreciated being named after his Father. He knew full well the privilege of being given such an excellent name.

I will remain in the world no longer,
but they are still in the world, and I am coming to you.
Holy Father, protect them by the power of your name–
the name you gave me–
so that they may be one as we are one.
While I was with them, I protected them
and kept them safe by the name you gave me.
John 17:11–12a

Jesus protected and kept his followers safe by the power of God's name. He asked his Father to continue to protect them by the power of that same name.

Oh, the power of that name! Even now Satan trembles at the thought of God's people ever coming to the full knowledge of the power in the name of Jesus. Could it be that this is precisely Satan's plan–one whose purpose is to keep us unskilled in the use of our mightiest spiritual weapon? How clever that Satan would have us take God's powerful name in vain, rather than appropriate it against Satan and his evil purposes. Is it any wonder this commandment has not been given the honor it deserves?

THE NAME OF GOD

In the days when our country was young, it was considered highly improper to speak lightly of God. God's name was regarded with utmost honor and dignity, much as one would address and elderly person with the respect due him or her. Never would you approach your elder on a first name basis and certainly never in terms of a nickname. Can you remember some of the names your grandparents used when referring to God?

The Maker The Supreme Being The Most High Jehovah
The Sovereign Providence The Father The Almighty

It was as though an aura of respect hovered over the name of God. People were careful, even cautious, when speaking his name. It appears our generation has lost that attitude of reverence. How sad that a healthy fear of God has been replaced by a commonness bordering on disrespect.

Jesus had a clear understanding of God's third commandment, "Thou shall not take the name of the Lord thy God in vain," and he very eloquently displayed the attitude we should have when approaching the name of his Father.

This, then, is how you should pray:
Our Father in heaven, hallowed be your name . . .
Matthew 6:9

Hallowed: Greek, hagiazo (hag-ee-ad'-zo): sacred, pure, blameless, consecrated, most holy

For "from the rising of the sun, even to its going down,
My name shall be great among the Gentiles;
in every place incense shall be offered to My name, and a pure offering;
for My name shall be great among the nations," says the Lord of hosts.
Malachi 1:11 (NKJV)

The earth may declare the glory of God—beast, fowl and fish may display God's splendor, but only man can speak and articulate, even dance to the greatness due God's name.

Because your love is better than life, my lips will glorify you.
I will praise you as long as I live,
and in your name I will lift up my hands.
Psalm 63:3–4

I SURRENDER

Some years back I taught the Bible curriculum at a local Christian school, grades 8–12. I smile when I remember the enthusiasm of those students, and I also recall a particular class discussion when the topic was worshipping the Lord. One of the many pubescent boys asked me, "Mrs. Menser, I don't understand about people raising their hands when they worship God. What's that all about?"

I had to be quick on my feet.

"If someone with a gun came into this room and pointed it at you, what would you do?" I asked.

"I'd put up my hands and show him I wasn't armed," he said.

"Would you wait a while to raise your hands?"

"Oh, no. I'd do it without even thinking."

"Why wouldn't you have to think about it?

"Because—he's more powerful than me and I want him to know I surrender to him."

I have seen you in the sanctuary and beheld your power and your glory.
Because your love is better than life, my lips will glorify you.
I will praise you as long as I live, and in your name I will lift up my hands.
My soul will be satisfied as with the richest of foods; with singing lips my mouth
will praise you. Praise the Lord. Sing to the Lord a new song,
his praise in the assembly of the saints.
Let Israel rejoice in their Maker; let the people of Zion be glad in their King.
Let them praise his name with dancing
and make music to him with tambourine and harp,
For the Lord takes delight in his people; he crowns the humble with salvation.
Let the saints rejoice in this honor and sing for joy on their beds.
Psalm 63:2–5, 149:2–5 (emphases mine)

Our lips were created to glorify God, so are our hands, mouth, and feet. There is a hallowed way in which to sing, dance, and make music unto the Lord. Yes, and because there is a hallowed way, there also isn't. But Scripture wouldn't tell us to express our praise to God, even that God takes delight in these expressions of praise, if these expressions were inherently disrespectful to his hallowed name. Scripture never contradicts itself, and so when Jesus instructs us to "hallow" the name of God, that does not exclude praising him with song, dance and the lifting of hands.

UPLIFTING OR CRUSHING?

You shall not take the name of
the Lord your God in vain.
Exodus 20:7a (NKJV)

Vain: Hebrew, *shav* (shawv): desolating, destructive, deceptive; falsely; uselessness

Remember how the enemy has mocked you, O Lord,
how foolish people have reviled your name.
They speak of you with evil intent;
your adversaries misuse your name.
Psalm 74:18, 139:20 (emphases mine)

Scripture tells us that enemies of God mock his name, foolish people revile his name, and that God considers those who misuse his name as his adversaries.

Sometimes you can understand the truest meaning of a word by pondering its opposite meaning. Interestingly, the opposite of the word "vain" is "useful" and "humble." These opposite words make it clear how we *should* refer to the name of God. Only with useful intent and a humble heart should we allow our mouths the privilege of speaking such an excellent, powerful name.

Recently my husband and I celebrated our wedding anniversary on the beautiful island of Aruba. We had a grand time and, no, you don't get any details! Except for one: every time the operator at the Hyatt Hotel answered our calls for room service, she always answered with the words, "Hello, Mrs. Menser, how may I help you, Mrs. Menser? Thank you, Mrs. Menser. Is there anything else I can help you with, Mrs. Menser?" The Hyatt staff was purposeful in speaking my name at every opportunity. I realized it was hotel protocol, but I liked it anyway. I also came to understand that I enjoyed hearing my name spoken in an Aruban accent and with intentional respect.

What does it say about the person who mispronounces or misspells your name? The obvious answer is they don't know you very well, or maybe not at all. There's no relationship here. And when you're in a crowd and no one even knows your name, how does that make you feel? Alone. Unimportant. Insignificant. The question begs to be asked, "How are we making God feel when we misuse his name?"

"You don't really know me." Alone.

"You don't appreciate me." Unimportant.

"You don't even see me." Insignificant.

The Name of God

PRINCIPLES

1. Jesus sought to glorify his Father's name, not build a name or reputation for himself.
2. Jesus hallowed/revered/respected the name of his Father.
3. Friends of God honor his name.
4. Obedience to God produces an excellent name.
5. Scripture teaches we are to praise the name of God with our entire being.
6. The name of Jesus provides salvation.
7. The name of Jesus releases the gift of the Holy Spirit.
8. The name of Jesus provides physical healing.
9. The name of Jesus produces signs and wonders.
10. The name of Jesus may cause you to suffer.
11. The name of Jesus may cause persecution and misunderstanding.
12. The name of Jesus enables men to preach boldly.
13. The name of Jesus has been reason for men to risk their lives.
14. The name of Jesus has the power to release people from demonic spirits.
15. The command to "not take the Lord's name in vain" was given by a Person who longs to be known.
16. The Lord will not hold the person guiltless who takes his name in vain.

The Name of God

DISCUSSION QUESTIONS

1. What are your thoughts about the specific behaviors Jesus exhibited that contributed to his excellent name (Philippians 2:7–11)?

2. Can you think of a person in your life who makes himself of no reputation, is a servant to others, and is humble and obedient? Write out the name of the person who comes to mind. You're a blessed person if lots of names come to mind.

3. It would be worth your time to take a moment to pray and ask God how you can be an encouragement to this person(s).

4. Some people believe it's irreverent to lift your hands in worship, or to sing and dance before the Lord. God's Word seems to indicate that it's irreverent behavior only when it's done irreverently. After studying this commandment, what are your thoughts about worshipping God?

5. Think about why the person who misuses God's name is referred to as God's enemy, his adversary, as well as being foolish. Write out a few of your thoughts.

6. How would you feel if, when someone was angry, in pain, or disgusted with a situation, they used *your* name to express their negative emotion? Fill in the blanks with your name.
   ________________________ Damn It!
   For ____________________________ Sake!
   My _____________________________!
   Oh My ______________________________!

7. How do you think it makes God feel when people speak his name in a vain manner?

8. After studying God's third commandment, my understanding of taking the Lord's name in vain is:

The works were finished from the foundation of the world.

Hebrews 4:3

Chapter 4
Remember the Sabbath
Exodus 20:8

"Don't Worry–God Rested."

There remains, then, a Sabbath-rest for the people of God. . .
Hebrews 4:9a

In this chapter you will learn . . .
- how anger and bitterness prohibit true Sabbath rest;
- why it's important to remember God's faithfulness when facing life's challenges;
- the historical context of when God provided our spiritual rest;
- characteristics of the hypocrite and the Pharisee.

Hebrew/Greek word studies: murmur, bitter, rest, Sabbath, therefore, unbelief, finished

The Sabbath is about much more than physical rest: it's about resting in God's faithfulness to meet all our needs. The highest purpose of the Sabbath is to remind us that we can spiritually rest because God has provided for all our needs. It is finished.

God wants us to rely on him, resting in the knowledge that he is in control of our lives and has provided for all our needs. The way of our flesh, however, is to be self-reliant: to work and perform and to try to prove our worth. It's a good thing the Bible tells us what do to with ourselves!

. . . for anyone who enters God's rest also rests from his own work, just as God did from his.
Hebrews 4:10

Jesus challenged the religious teachers' understanding of the meaning of the Sabbath. This challenge shook the foundation of their religious activities. These leaders had, by their own acts of righteousness, attained an envious level of respectability in their communities. Now this uneducated Nazarene was offering them a religion based on God's provision of love, mercy, and grace. Jesus was *giving the gift of the Sabbath*, while the teachers of the law preferred to earn their status with God and with man.

Sabbath rest came to Jesus as he relieved others of their distress. For Jesus, the fulfilling of the command to "keep the Sabbath" included: providing food for the hungry, health to a shriveled hand, and healing to the back of a woman crippled with pain. For today's believer, the Sabbath is a day we should revere as we reflect on the encompassing provisions of an awesome and compassionate Creator.

REMEMBER THE SABBATH

What are your first thoughts when you hear those words, "Remember the Sabbath"? Since we're in the process of learning about the Sabbath, it seems only fitting to return to our Hebrew ancestors and observe their circumstances when God was teaching them what it meant to keep the Sabbath. We'll recall God's people had been living as slaves in the land of Egypt. Miraculously, they were set free and on their way to worship God in a land he had promised them. Along the way their lips became parched and their bellies empty, resulting in a growing discontentment toward the leaders who had led them to this dry land.

In the desert the whole community grumbled against Moses and Aaron.
Exodus 16:2

So they were in the desert. Grumbling. Against Moses and Aaron.

Grumbled/Murmured: Hebrew, *luwn* (loon): to be obstinate, to complain continually

The entire community of Israelites was blaming Moses and Aaron for their hunger and thirst. Their complaints were continual . . . actually dripping with discontent.

The Israelites said to them, "If only we had died by the Lord's hand in Egypt!
There we sat around pots of meat and ate all the food we wanted,
but you have brought us out into this desert to starve this entire assembly to death."
We remember the fish we ate in Egypt at no cost–
also the cucumbers, melons, leeks, onions and garlic.
Exodus 16:3, Numbers 11:5 (emphasis mine)

Hunger was their specific complaint. These newly released slaves were remembering meals eaten in Egypt while forgetting their lifetime of slavery to a ruthless taskmaster. And now their stomachs ached for the familiar Egyptian food.

Though freed from Egypt, these Hebrews maintained a slave mentality. Slavery had distorted their thinking. Cucumbers, melons, leeks, onions and garlic were all they knew. And they even thought this pittance of food was given to them at no cost. No cost? Four hundred years of slavery sounds like a high price to pay for that menu.

God wanted more for them.

So I have come down to rescue them from the hand of the Egyptians
and to bring them up out of that land into a good and spacious land,
a land flowing with milk and honey.
Exodus 3:8

Much more.

When they reached the Valley of Eshcol,
they cut off a branch bearing a single cluster of grapes.
Two of them carried it on a pole between them,
along with some pomegranates and figs.
Numbers 13:23

Leeks, onions and garlic—or milk and honey, clusters of grapes so large it takes two men to carry them, pomegranates and figs? I know which platter I'd choose.

When hunger hit, the Hebrews were quick to want to return to the familiar and forfeit the delicacies God had prepared for them. Moses heard their grumbling . . . Aaron heard their grumbling . . . but, most important, God heard their grumbling.

Then the Lord said to Moses:
"I have heard the grumbling of the Israelites.
Tell them, 'At twilight you will eat meat,
and in the morning you will be filled with bread.
Then you will know that I am the Lord your God.'"
Exodus 16:11–12

So, they're eating meat and manna. Bellies are full. But God knows they're suffering from a much greater malady than hunger. There is a deeper source to their discontent.

Bear in mind that the Lord has given you the Sabbath:
that is why on the sixth day he gives you bread for two days.
Everyone is to stay where he is on the seventh day; no one is to go out."
So the people rested on the seventh day.
Exodus 16: 29–30 (emphases mine)

He said to them, "This is what the Lord commanded:
'Tomorrow is to be a day of rest, a holy Sabbath to the Lord.
So bake what you want to bake and boil what you want to boil.
Save whatever is left and keep it until morning.' "
So they saved it until morning, as commanded,
and it did not stink or get maggots in it.
"Eat it today," Moses said, "because today is a Sabbath to the Lord.
You will not find any of it on the ground today. Six days you are to gather it,
but on the seventh day, the Sabbath, there will not be any."
Nevertheless, some of the people went out on the seventh day to gather it,
but they found none. Then the Lord said to Moses,
"How long will you refuse to keep my commands and my instructions?

Bear in mind that the Lord has given you the Sabbath. . ."
Exodus 16:23–28a (emphases mine)

Stay with me here. We're about to connect some important Sabbath dots.

On the seventh day there would be no manna.

Nevertheless some of the Hebrews still went out looking for manna.

God's response to Moses was:

"How long will you refuse to keep my commands and my instructions?
Bear in mind that the Lord has given you the Sabbath. . ."
Exodus 16:28–29a (emphasis mine)

Moses is told to remember the Lord has given him the Sabbath. Really? How is he supposed to remember that? The Ten Commandments hadn't been written yet. This doesn't happen until Exodus, Chapter 20. So how can God expect Moses to remember the Sabbath?

It's the *principle of the Sabbath* to which God is referring. This is a vital dot that must be connected in order to see the big picture of what it means to "keep the Sabbath." Genesis comes *before* Exodus. Note that God sanctified the seventh day in Genesis, long before he ever gave Moses the Ten Commandments in Exodus.

Thus the heavens and the earth, and all the host of them, were finished,
and on the seventh day God ended His work which he had done,
and he rested on the seventh day from all his work which he had done.
Then God blessed the seventh day and sanctified it,
because in it he rested from all his work which God had created and made.
Genesis 2:1–3 (KJV)

Sanctified: Hebrew, *qadash* (kaw-dash'): to make, pronounce, observe as clean; to dedicate, to consecrate, to purify, to proclaim hallow

The highest purpose of the Sabbath is to remind us of the finished work of God. Remembering the Sabbath should cause us to have faith in a God who has provided for every need his creations would demand. Genesis 2:1–

3 tells us that God forgot nothing: all was finished. All means all, including the needs of the Hebrew children, found in Exodus, Chapter 16.

Let's not stop until we understand *why* God told his children not to gather food on the seventh day. It's not about food. God can handle providing food. God wanted them to trust he had *already* provided for their needs. Observe the sequence of God's creative process and how it suggests God provided for man before he even created man:

1st day–light
2nd day–sky
3rd day–dry land and vegetation
4th day–sun, moon and stars
5th day–birds and sea creatures
6th day–livestock, wild animals, crawling creatures and mankind

Remembering the Sabbath is about having faith that God has looked fully into our future and provided for us before he even created us. Think about it. Why didn't God create man first? Because man would be without light to live by and land to grow food upon. There would be no sun, moon and stars to determine the seasons. Birds, fish, and livestock wouldn't be in place to provide nourishment for him. God provided for man before he created man.

Back to our Hebrew ancestors. Would they believe God could keep their meat and manna fresh for that one extra day? Some could not, and so they went about working, planning, stockpiling their manna just in case God couldn't be trusted, didn't remember them, didn't care or wasn't able to provide. Once again, fear that God would not provide led these faithless Hebrews down a path of unbelief.

Now faith is being sure of what we hope for and certain of what we do not see.
This is what the ancients were commended for.
By faith we understand that the universe was formed at God's command,
so that what is seen was not made out of what was visible.
<u>And without faith it is impossible to please God</u>. . .
Hebrews 11:1, 6a (emphasis mine)

Faith is a big deal to God. It's a foundational principle reflecting who he is and what pleases him. Faith asks, "Do you know me? Do you believe I'm good? Do you believe I love you enough to provide for you? Do you know that I provided for you before I even created you? If, by faith, you don't know these things about me, then I am not pleased, because you really don't know me. And knowing me is why I created you."

IT'S ALL ABOUT FAITH

Then the Lord said to Moses,
"Tell the Israelites to turn back and encamp near Pi Hahiroth, between Migdol and the sea. They are to encamp by the sea,
directly opposite Baal Zephon.
Pharaoh will think,
'The Israelites are wandering around the land in confusion,
hemmed in by the desert. And I will harden Pharaoh's heart,
and he will pursue them.
But I will gain glory for myself through Pharaoh and all his army,
and the Egyptians will know that I am the Lord.
So the Israelites did this.
Exodus 14:1–4 (emphasis mine)

That's the set up.
Here's the point:

Pharaoh thought the Israelites left Egypt in confusion. Yet scripture tell us the Israelites were "marching boldly" in their exodus from Egypt.

The Lord hardened the heart of Pharaoh king of Egypt,
so that he pursued the Israelites who were marching out boldly.
Exodus 14:8 (emphasis mine)

At least that's how they began their journey. Boldly. Boldly until they saw Pharaoh's horses, chariots, horsemen and troops pursuing them.

As Pharaoh approached, the Israelites looked up,
and there were the Egyptians, marching after them.
They were terrified and cried out to the Lord. They said to Moses,

"Was it because there were no graves in Egypt that you brought us to the desert to die?"
Exodus 14:10-11a

From marching boldly to being terrified. Been there done that.

Then Moses answered the terrified cries of the Israelites.

"Do not be afraid.
Stand firm and you will see the deliverance the Lord will bring to you today.
The Egyptians you see today you will never see again.
The Lord will fight for you; you need only to be still."
Exodus 14:13-14

Still: Hebrew, *charash* (khaw-rash'): to be silent, to let alone, cease, leave off speaking, hold peace, be quiet, rest

But the Israelites went through the sea on dry ground,
with a wall of water on their right and on their left. That day the Lord saved Israel from the hands of the Egyptians,
and Israel saw the Egyptians lying dead on the shore.
And when the Israelites saw the great power the Lord displayed against the Egyptians,
the people feared the Lord and put their trust in him and in Moses his servant.
Exodus 14:29-31(emphasis mine)

From fearing Pharaoh to fearing God. That's what happens when we remember the Sabbath, get still, and put our trust in God.

GETTING RID OF BITTERNESS

Following the parting of the sea and seeing the Egyptians lying dead on the shore, the Hebrews were faced with the challenge of traveling three days in the wilderness without water. When they did find water, it was neither sweet nor refreshing. But even though the water was initially bitter and of no use to them, it did provide a means whereby God could teach them a great kingdom principle.

For three days they traveled in the desert without finding water.
When they came to Marah, they could not drink its water because it was bitter.
Exodus 15:22b-23a

Bitter: Hebrew, *marah* (maw-raw'): to be angry, to be grieved, to be vexed

Living their entire lives as slaves, forced day after day after day to endure hard physical labor, parents and grandparents, now dead, having never tasted any semblance of freedom, understandably, the Hebrews had tentacles of bitterness that went deep, rooted in the soil of slavery and injustice. They were *generationally* bitter—and they needed to be healed.

The Israelites were angry. In Egypt, they'd felt alone and forgotten. Painful memories filled their minds and a lingering taste of resentment had settled in their spirits. Though physically free from Egypt, their emotions remained shackled to the past. They were the "wandering wounded," and it was all so hard to bear. Mercifully, God knew that before the Israelites could receive the blessings of their Promised Land, they needed to unload the injustices of their bitter past. And God used a piece of wood to accomplish this.

Then Moses cried out to the Lord, and the Lord showed him a piece of wood.
He threw it into the water, and the water became sweet.
Exodus 15:25 (emphasis mine)

Once again, the Hebrews were at the mercy of God. There was nothing they could do to heal the water they so desperately needed. Their problem required divine intervention, and so the Divine intervened. Using a piece of wood, God brought sweetness to that which was bitter. In doing this, God pointed the way to another piece of wood, fashioned in the shape of a cross where, one day, his people could lay down all their mistreatment, regrets, bitterness and pain in exchange for his sweet, life-giving water. And isn't it true today that we must come to that same understanding: that the *only* place where the injustices of our past can be made sweet, forgiveness complete, and healing received is at the foot of a piece of wood?

Perhaps you're at the same point in your life as were the Hebrew children. Are you determined to leave Egypt, taking your family and finances with you? Now, do you find yourself at the banks of a Great Sea with the dust of Pharaoh's army following closely behind? Are you afraid, tempted to return to the only lifestyle you've ever known? Has bitterness found a place in your heart? Do you find yourself grumbling and wondering if God even cares?

Before answering those questions, let's address a more important one: *Has the blood of the Lamb been applied to your doorpost?* This is where your journey to freedom begins. For without the covering of the blood of the Lamb, your *spirit* remains dead in the land of Egypt, imprisoned, slave to a taskmaster, and not yet set free to seek your Promised Land.

On that same night I will pass through Egypt
and strike down every firstborn–both men and animals–
and I will bring judgment on all the gods of Egypt.
I am the Lord.
The blood will be a sign for you on the houses where you are;
and when I see the blood, I will pass over you.
Exodus 12:12-13a

God sees the blood of the lamb: death passes over you.

God does not see the blood of the lamb: death and judgment are your fate.

If you've accepted the blood of the Lamb as your means of life and liberty but you find yourself in the same place as the Hebrews when they were on the way to their Promised Land, then these questions are relevant:

Do you want to leave Egypt?
Do want to take your family and finances with you?
Are you between an enemy and an overwhelming sea?
Are you tempted to return to your former lifestyle?
Has bitterness found a home in your heart?
Do you find yourself grumbling and wondering if God even cares?

Don't give up! Please don't give up. You're not alone in these feelings. If God could deliver over 600,000 Hebrew slaves from a land full of bitter injustices, he can surely take care of you. Remember that *God allowed* Pharaoh to follow his children, and you might have a pharaoh following you, but it will be your faith in God that will sustain you to move beyond your bitter injustices and fear of the future, forward, to your Promised

Land. God has provided all you'll need for this journey. And remember, it's not all up to you.

REST TAKES EFFORT

We shouldn't be too hard on our Hebrew ancestors who, while in the midst of a crisis, forgot the sufficiency of their God. How often do we forget God's awesome power, particularly when life throws us an unexpected curve? For a review of the importance of "Remembering the Sabbath," let's return to the place where the Sabbath was birthed.

1st day—light
2nd day—sky
3rd day—dry land and vegetation
4th day—sun, moon and stars
5th day—birds and sea creatures
6th day—livestock, wild animals, crawling creatures and mankind

At this point, God's work was finished.

Thus the heavens and the earth, and all the host of them, were finished.
And on the seventh day God ended His work which He had done,
and He rested on the seventh day from all His work which He had done.
Then God blessed the seventh day and sanctified it,
and He rested on the seventh day from all the work which He had done.
Genesis 2:1-3 (NKJV)

Rested: Hebrew, *shabath* (shaw-bath'): to repose, to desist from exertion, to cease, to celebrate, to rid, to put away, to be still
Sanctified: Hebrew, *qadash* (kaw-dash'): to make or pronounce clean, to proclaim holy

And yet his work has been finished since the creation of the world.
For somewhere he has spoken about the seventh day in these words:
"And on the seventh day God rested from all his work."
For in six days the Lord made heaven and earth, the sea, and all that is in them,
But he rested on the seventh day.
Therefore, the Lord blessed the Sabbath day and made it holy.
Hebrews 4:3b-4. Exodus 20:11

Sabbath: Hebrew, *shabbath* (shab-bawth′): intermission; to repose, to desist from exertion

God even provided the means for our salvation "from the creation of the world":

All inhabitants of the earth will worship the beast–
all whose names have not been written in the book of life
belonging to the Lamb that was slain from the creation of the world.
He who has an ear, let him hear.
Revelation 13:8 (emphasis mine)

It takes faith to believe God provided for all of our needs from the days of creation, even to the provision of a Lamb who would one day be slain for our sins. But remember, God is all about faith. God loves seeing his children have faith in him, his love and good will toward us. Above all, remember that . . .

Without faith it is impossible to please God.
Hebrews 11:6a

During Jesus' ministry on earth there was a boy who was possessed by an evil spirit. This spirit robbed him of his speech and would throw him to the ground. The boy would foam at the mouth and gnash with his teeth, and his body would become rigid. The father of the boy spoke of times when this spirit would actually throw his son into fire or water in order to kill him! The father asked Jesus' disciples to drive out the spirit, but they were unable to do so.

"O unbelieving generation," Jesus replied . . .
Mark 9:19a

"But if you can do anything, take pity on us and help us," begged the boy's father (Mark 9:22b).
" 'If you can'?" said Jesus. "Everything is possible for him who believes" (Mark 9:23).
"I do believe," replied the father. "Help me overcome my unbelief" (In Mark 9:24b).

Unbelief: Greek, *apaistia* (ap-is-tee′-ah): faithlessness, disbelief

The words of this father aptly describe the lives of many believers. We have a measure of belief—but it's mixed with unbelief. Such was the plight of this concerned father. The father believed, yet he knew he needed more belief. He had some faith, yet Jesus described his generation as "faithless."

Jesus' disciples weren't above finding themselves in this same dilemma of faithlessness.

The apostles said to the Lord,
"Increase our faith!"
Luke 17:5

The early generation of Hebrews needed faith to believe God would provide for their necessities of life. The apostles and the father of the possessed boy needed faith to believe Jesus was able to provide a miracle of healing.

So how does a person actually get faith?

So then, faith comes by hearing, and hearing by the word of God.
Romans 10:17 (NKJV)

Hearing God's Word>>>increases our faith>>>which drives out unbelief.

Still, many of us won't take the time to study God's Word and hear the voice of God for ourselves. We lack faith because we haven't fed ourselves the Word of faith. Even though God continually calls us to spend time with him, to get to know him, to build our faith through prayer and reading his Word, we all too often drown out his invitation with the desires of our own hearts. The result is that we walk in fear and unbelief when a life of faith is clearly within our reach.

We need to be told that God *likes* us and enjoys spending time with us. Oh, he may not like everything we do, but God is very capable of separating us from our sins. God sees all of who we are and who we will become. Remember, God created us in his own image, and when he looks at us, he smiles and says, "Very good" (Gen. 1:31). God loves us and, as our Friend, he *wants* to spend time with us. Friends want to be together. It's not a duty to be with someone you love. It's a delight!

BY FAITH

Hebrews, Chapter 11 . . .

- v. 3: They understood that the universe was formed at God's command.
- v. 4: Abel offered God a better sacrifice than his brother, Cain, did.
- v. 5: Enoch did not experience death, because God took him away.
- v. 7: Noah built an ark when as yet the earth had never seen rain.
- v. 8b: Abraham obeyed and went . . . when he didn't even know here he was going.
- v. 11–12: Sarah received strength to conceive because she judged him faithful who had promised.
- v. 17: Abraham offered up Isaac as a sacrifice to God.
- v. 23: Moses' parents hid him for three months and were not afraid of the king's command.
- v. 24–25: Moses refused to be known as the son of Pharaoh's daughter, choosing instead to be mistreated along with the people of God.
- v. 27: Moses left Egypt, not fearing the wrath of the king.
- v. 29: The Israelites passed through the Red Sea.
- v. 30: The walls of Jericho fell.
- v. 35: Women received back their dead.
- v. 35: Others were enabled to endure torture.
- v. 37: Some were sawed in two, and some were put to death by the sword.
- v. 37–38: Still others were destitute, persecuted and mistreated, wandering in deserts and mountains, in caves and in holes.

These were all commended for their faith,
yet none of them received what had been promised.
God had planned something better for us
so that only together with us would they be made perfect.
Therefore, since we are surrounded by such a great cloud of witnesses,
let us throw off everything that hinders and the sin that so easily entangles,
and let us run with perseverance the race marked out for us.
Hebrews 11:40, 12:1

Faithful witnesses, continually in the presence of God, crucifying their fleshly desires, choosing to live by the Spirit–such were these beautiful "clouds" who are now looking to us to perfect what was promised to them. These seven words are used to describe them:

The world was not worthy of them.
Hebrews 11:38a

JESUS KEPT THE SABBATH

Rest can take many forms. There's a rest that comes after a good night's sleep, and there's a rest enjoyed when we've completed a task. Rest can mean a walk on a beach or a few minutes with your favorite book. Rest brings relief from weariness and a freedom from worry. Rest can be refreshing to our flesh or our spirit and sometimes to both!

As Christians, we can look to Jesus as our example of how to experience Sabbath rest. Ironically, what gave Jesus rest and delight seemed to provoke frustration in the lives of his "religious" peers.

One Sabbath Jesus was going through the grainfields, and his disciples
began to pick some heads of grain,
rub them in their hands and eat the kernels.
Some of the Pharisees asked,
"Why are you doing what is unlawful on the Sabbath?"
Luke 6:1–2

- The disciples picked grain on the Sabbath.
- The Pharisees thought picking grain on the Sabbath was unlawful.

On another Sabbath he went into the synagogue and was teaching,
and a man was there whose right hand was shriveled.
The Pharisees and the teachers of the law
were looking for a reason to accuse Jesus,
so they watched him closely to see if he would heal on the Sabbath.
He looked around at them all, and then said to the man,
"Stretch out your hand."

He did so, and his hand was completely restored.
But they were furious and began to discuss with one another
what they might do to Jesus.
Luke 6:6–7, 10–11

- Jesus healed a man's hand on the Sabbath.
- The Pharisees thought healing a man's hand on the Sabbath was unlawful.

On a Sabbath Jesus was teaching in one of the synagogues,
and a woman was there who had been crippled by a spirit for eighteen years.
She was bent over and could not straighten up at all.
When Jesus saw her, he called her forward and said to her,
"Woman, you are set free from your infirmity."
Then he put his hands on her,
and immediately she straightened up and praised God.
Indignant because Jesus had healed on the Sabbath,
the synagogue ruler said to the people,
"There are six days for work. So come and be healed on those days,
not on the Sabbath."
Luke 13:10–14 (emphasis mine)

- Jesus healed a woman from her infirmity on the Sabbath.
- The Pharisees were indignant because Jesus healed a woman's infirmity on the Sabbath.

Jesus' rest came when he relieved others of their distress. For Jesus, the fulfilling of his Father's command to "keep the Sabbath" included: *providing* food for the hungry, *providing* health to a shriveled hand, and *providing* healing to the back of a woman crippled with pain. For today's believer, the Sabbath is a day to revere as we reflect on the encompassing provisions of our Creator.

Yes, the Sabbath is *both* a day and a lifestyle. It is a day in that God tells us to set it aside, rest, and focus on his faithfulness. Isaiah, the prophet, indicates it's a day we will enjoy even in Heaven!

"As the new heavens and the new earth that I make will endure before me," declares the Lord, "so will your name and descendants endure. From one New Moon to another and <u>from one Sabbath to another</u>, all mankind will come and bow down before me," says the Lord.
Isaiah 66:22–23 (emphasis mine)

And it's a lifestyle indicative of the people of God.

There remains, then, a Sabbath-rest for the people of God: for anyone who enters God's rest also <u>rests from his own work</u>, just as God did from his. Let us, therefore, make every effort to enter that rest. . .
Hebrews 4:11a (emphasis mine)

How sad that the religious leaders of Jesus' day refused to grasp the truest meaning of the Sabbath. Was it their training in the laws of Moses which caused them to resist the teachings of Jesus? Note that eventually their questions regarding the Sabbath evolved into emotions of fury and indignation and that, ultimately, the Pharisees sentenced Jesus to die on a cross due to his actions of love on the Sabbath.

Jesus challenged the Pharisees' doctrine of the meaning of the Sabbath. This challenge shook the foundation of their religious reputations; for up to now the religious leaders had, by their own acts of righteousness, attained an envious level of respectability in their communities. Now this uneducated Nazarene was offering them a religion based on grace. Jesus was *giving* the gift of the Sabbath, while the Pharisees and teachers of the law preferred to *earn* their status with God and man. Jesus had warned his disciples of the erroneous, misguided, dangerous teaching of the Pharisees.

"Be on your guard against the yeast of the Pharisees, which is <u>hypocrisy</u>."
Luke 12:1b

<u>Hypocrisy</u>: Greek, *hupokrisis* (hoop-ok'-ree-sis): acting under a feigned part, speaking or acting under a false part; to pretend

"You hypocrites!
Isaiah was right when he prophesied about you:
" 'These people honor me with their lips, but their hearts are far from me.
They worship me in vain; their teachings are but rules taught by man.' "
Matthew 15:7-9

Jesus drew a strong comparison between a hypocrite and a Pharisee in Matthew, Chapter 23:

- v.3: They do not practice what they preach.
- v.4: They tie up heavy loads and put them on men's shoulders.
- v.5: Everything they do is for men to see.
- v.6: They love the place of honor at banquets and the most important seats in the synagogues.
- v.7: They love to be greeted in the marketplaces and to have men call them "Rabbi."
- v.27: They are like whitewashed tombs which look beautiful on the outside but on the inside are full of dead men's bones and everything unclean.
- v.28: In the same way, on the outside they appear to be righteous, but on the inside they are full of hypocrisy and wickedness.

One person may not exhibit every trait of a Pharisee. Jesus, however, wanted no trace of the Pharisees' leaven living in his people. Jesus further described Pharisees as hypocrites, descendants of murderers, snakes, a brood of vipers, and blind guides (Matthew, Chapter 23). Jesus warns us to beware of the person who carries within him the slow-moving, permeating yeast of the Pharisees.

A common characteristic of the Pharisee is that he is approval-oriented and will publicly deceive others in order to gain the applause of family, friends, and especially those he greets in the workplace. Performing seems quite natural to the Pharisee, as he appears more at ease on stage before men than at rest in the intimate presence of God.

What a wearisome lifestyle, for, as the Pharisee continues to perform—perform—perform, his flesh is slowly being drained of its limited energy and resources. The controlled, calculated abilities of the flesh have proven to be incapable of sustaining in the Pharisee the power and "joy unspeakable" Scripture says are rightfully his (1 Peter 1:8). The Pharisee can now be recognized by the frown on his face, the crease in his brow, and the critical words of his tongue. You see, the Pharisee is tired, overloaded and overworked. It's a self-inflicted fatigue. Eventually the Pharisee will cry out, "I'm exhausted. No one is helping me. I'm doing God's work all by myself." And in some ways, he's exactly right.

Why does the Pharisee put himself in such a burdensome position? Why is it so hard for him to trust anyone other than himself? Why can't he rest? And look out: for once a Pharisee becomes suspicious of losing control, he'll simultaneously become distrustful of those around him who don't offer their accolades and applause.

Stephen and the Sanhedrin

by Pat Menser
Acts, Chapter 7

Stephen was a man of God who longed to serve his Lord,
In freedom, truth and reverence, in praise and one accord.
His message was a cry for change from rituals and rites,
To turn their hearts to Jesus, the Savior and True Light.

But envy gripped these men of cloth as they watched Stephen perform
God's signs and wonders—miracles—not seen in church before.
"How dare he change our customs? Who *does* he think he is?"
"We'll find a testimony who is witness to his sin!"

You see, the law of Moses was well-known—its message fully learned.
But now the song of grace and love was longing to be heard.
But some priests can be hard-hearted, the Sanhedrin—stiff and cold.
"We learned these rules in school," they say. "It's what we have been told!"

Soon their envy turned to fury, and they gnashed their teeth at him.
"How dare he say we disobeyed the laws God gave to men?"
Then they refused the Holy Spirit as their fathers had before,
When they persecuted prophets for predicting of our Lord.

They dragged Stephen from the city, and they beat him with their stones,
Refusing his free message that their sins had been atoned.
And while they were killing Stephen—he looked to God above,
He prayed they'd be forgiven, then he fell asleep in love.

Jesus said, "Father, forgive them, for they do not know what they are doing."
Luke 23:34a

A Pharisee doesn't see that, through Jesus, God offers rest–relief from his life of performance and perfection. Instead of receiving this gift of rest, the Pharisee prefers to cling violently, indignantly to the yeast which protects his reputation and applauds his good works. This is an insidious yeast with which Jesus was well acquainted. For, you see, it's the yeast of the Pharisees–"salvation by works of the flesh"–which beat, scourged, and then nailed the "gift of the Sabbath" to a cross.

Would death bring an end to this Nazarene? Can we please return to our rules and rituals?

After the Sabbath, at dawn on the first day of the week,
Mary Magdalene and the other Mary went to look at the tomb.
The angel said to the women, "Do not be afraid,
for I know that you are looking for Jesus, who was crucified,
He is not here; he has risen, just as he said."
Matthew 28:1, 5–6a (emphasis mine)

It was God's sovereign will that the yeast of hypocrisy and self-righteousness would crucify the Son of God–but it was only part of his plan. For God had determined that in three days his gift of grace would rise far above the yeast that had sought to destroy it. GRACE HAS RISEN!

Sabbath

PRINCIPLES

1. The highest purpose of the Sabbath is to remind us of the finished work of God.
2. Our salvation was provided from the foundations of the world.
3. We can rest because God finished his work.
4. Hearing God's Word increases our faith and drives out unbelief.
5. Grumbling is an indicator of fear and lack of faith.
6. God not only wants to save us from our sins, he wants to heal us of the bitterness from our past.
7. Jesus' example of Sabbath rest produced indignation in the Pharisees.
8. The Pharisee is more at ease performing for men than resting with God.
9. It's a choice to rest in God.
10. It takes effort to rest in God.
11. Sabbath rest results in reliance upon God to meet all our needs.
12. When we desist, cease, put away and rid ourselves of worry, works and exertion, we proclaim God's Sabbath in us.
13. The Word of God + Faith in God = Rest in God.

Sabbath

DISCUSSION QUESTIONS

1. What are some reasons the activities of Pharisees are generally applauded by our society?

2. Why did the Hebrews accuse Moses of bringing them into the desert? (Exodus 16:3b)

3. Against whom, did Moses say, were their accusations really aimed? (Exodus 16:7b–8a)

4. When faced with life's challenges, why do we often want to return to the familiar rather than move forward?

5. Why is it an effort to enter God's rest?

6. Why do many Christians *not* enjoy Sabbath rest?

7. Why is an understanding of what it means to "Remember the Sabbath" vital to your spiritual foundation?

8. What must you do to enter God's rest? (Hebrews 4:10)

9. What word describes the Christian who doesn't enter God's rest? (Hebrews 4:11)

10. Why must faith precede rest?

11. How is a person's faith increased?

12. What is the biggest challenge you're facing today?

13. Reflect on a specific time when God brought you through your personal "Red Sea."

14. On a scale of 1–10, circle the number indicating where you are in the process of entering God's rest—10 means you are super-rested!
    1 2 3 4 5 6 7 8 9 10

And Jesus grew in wisdom and stature, and in favor with God and men.

Luke 2:52

Chapter 5

Honor Your Parents

Exodus 20:12

"It Takes Humility."

In this chapter you will read about . . .

- Jesus' attitude toward his earthly parents and how he honored both them and his heavenly Father;
- the reasons why the benefit of a long life is related to the command to honor one's parents;
- the role faith played in Abraham's ability to honor God with his son;
- Abraham and Rebekah's contrasting parenting styles.

Hebrew/Greek word studies: subject, wisdom, stature, favor, honor, meek/lowly, disobedience, train

Luke 2:41–52 tells the story of twelve-year-old Jesus exercising his free will in order to follow the perfect will of his heavenly Father. Though his decision was unpopular with his parents, Jesus chose to walk the road that was true to his person. Jesus let nothing interfere with his flint-like determination to do the will of his Father, not even the threat of being misunderstood by his parents. The Bible teaches there were times when Mary and Joseph didn't understand some of their son's choices. Jesus' response to his parent's confusion was:

"Why were you searching for me?" he asked.
"Didn't you know I had to be in my Father's house?"
Luke 2:49

Parents can teach their young children to honor them and should expect submission to their authority. As children begin to mature, however, parents must mature as well. Parents must recognize that, as their children grow toward adulthood, they're capable of hearing the voice of God for themselves. As children become adults, their first allegiance should be to obey the voice of their heavenly Parent.

Surely I was sinful at birth, sinful from the time my mother conceived me.
As for you, you were dead in your transgressions and sins,
in which you used to live when you followed the ways of this world and of the ruler of the kingdom of the air,
the spirit who is now at work in those who are disobedient.
Psalm 51:5, Ephesians 2:1–2

Before the blood of the Lamb covered our sins, our spirit was dead and our hearts were hard. God called us "children of disobedience."

Disobedient: Greek, *apeitheia* (ap-i′-thi-ah): obstinate, unpersuadable, pig-headed, puffed up, rebellious, arrogant, contrary, defiant

That is what we all were before we became children of God.
But this is *not* how God wants us to remain.

Honor your father and your mother,
so that you may live long in the land the Lord your God is giving you.
Children, obey your parents in the Lord, for this is right.
"Honor your father and mother"–which is the first commandment with a promise–
"that it may go well with you and that you may enjoy long life on earth."
Exodus 20:12, Ephesians 6:1–3

"How much farther?" he asked.

"Soon we will take rest," the father replied.

"But Father, I am weary, and thirsty . . . very thirsty. And hunger is upon me. Have we any leeks or onions from home?"

"In haste we were summoned to leave. Did your mother not bring dough from the trough before the yeast could be added? We must not grow weary as we follow Jehovah to our Promised Land. He will give us strength to continue."

"Father, the flocks and the herds . . . they too desire food and water."

"Jehovah is able to provide for our needs. He shall water the herds as well as the people. No more complaining, my son."

Several hours passed, and as the noonday sun branded its heat upon the young child. He soon forgot his father's words.

"Oh father, I am so thirsty! Where are we going? Will there be food there when we arrive?"

"My son, my son, we are going to a land promised to father Abraham and to our leader, Moses. Have I not taught you to remember the Sabbath and the promise it holds? We must have faith, my son, that all is provided."

"I heard talk we are going by way of the desert. Is that not a very long journey?" the child asked.

"Your ears hear much to be so young. Yes, the cloud moves by way of the wilderness. It is Jehovah who leads the way. We must follow the path he has chosen," the father explained.

"But, Father, why does the cloud not find its way to water and food? I am thirsty and I am hungry, and I want to go home."

* * * * *

Can you fathom an exodus of six hundred thousand men, along with their wives and children? Moses' task of freeing the Hebrew children and leading them to their Promised Land was overwhelming. Add to these numbers the fact that for over four hundred years the Israelites had known only a lifestyle of slavery, a lifestyle where all their decisions were made for them–when and where to work, when and what to eat–and now they were free? Free, but perhaps feeling more lost than ever. How do you *do* "free" when you've never experienced freedom or seen it lived out in any of your relationships?

It seems one of the first lessons God had to teach the Israelites was that freedom from bondage wouldn't mean freedom from hardship. Scripture doesn't reveal the words or the thoughts of the Hebrew children involved in this freedom pilgrimage, and so we can only imagine the conversations that took place between the Hebrew parents and their sons and daughters. What we do know, however, is that these children saw more of God's power in their young lives than we'll see in a lifetime. Plagues of frogs, boils, gnats and flies, a congealed sea separated to allow passage on dry ground, an Egyptian army swallowed up by the same sea, a pillar of cloud by day and fire by night: mighty miracles to be seen by such little eyes. And now, after all the miraculous dust had settled, the children, the parents, the flocks and the herds, though free from Egypt, were thirsty and so very hungry.

In the desert the whole community grumbled against Moses and Aaron.
Exodus 16:2

The *whole* Hebrew community grumbled about the direction their lives were taking. It seems their endeavor to build new lives for themselves and their families proved to be more of a challenge than they'd anticipated. Hardship was upon them, making it difficult to accept it was God's will for them to be in their present condition.

MISUNDERSTOOD OBEDIENCE

Conceived in the womb of an unmarried Jewish girl, birthed in the smell of straw and manure, reared in the modest home of a carpenter, submissive to his parents and soft-spoken to his fellow man: meekness was the birthmark of Jesus. And though their home was modest, their means meager, Mary and Joseph brought great richness into the life of their son by teaching him to "honor your father and your mother." It was a commandment that would find its most difficult fulfillment on a wooden cross.

Honor your father and your mother,
that your days may be long upon the land which the Lord your God is giving you.
Then He went down with them
and came to Nazareth, and was subject to them. . .
Exodus 20:12, Luke 2:51a (NKJV)

Honor: Hebrew, *kebed* (kaw-bad'): to be heavy (in a good sense), to be chargeable
"Honor suggests a combination of liking and respect." (*Random House Dictionary*)
Subject: Greek, *hupotasso* (hoop-ot-as'-so): an inferior position; to submit self unto, to be under obedience, to place beneath

Available to us today are the same commandments Mary and Joseph taught Jesus. We can teach our children to honor us, and we should expect submission to our authority. As our children begin to mature, however, we must mature as well. We must recognize that our children are growing up and gradually becoming more and more capable of hearing the voice of God for themselves. It's then that we would be wise to encourage a "transfer of obedience" to take place. This concept implies that, as children become adults, their first allegiance should no longer be to us, their parents, but rather to God. Recall Jesus' defense to staying behind in Jerusalem when his parents expected him to follow them back home.

So when they saw Him, they were amazed; and His mother said to Him,
"Son, why have You done this to us?
Look, Your father and I have sought You anxiously."
And He said to them, "Why did you seek Me?
Did you not know that I must be about My Father's business?"
Luke 2:48–49 (NKJV)

So how do we honor our parents while at the same time obey the voice of God—particularly when the two seem to disagree with one another? This is the dilemma young Jesus faced. Perhaps the actions of the twelve-year-old Nazarene will give us insight into what the commandment, "Honor your father and your mother," truly means.

Luke 2:41-51

- v. 41: Jesus' parents went to Jerusalem every year. This indicates the journey had been made before and was a family tradition. Jesus knew the routine well and what his parents expected of him.
- v. 42: Jesus is now twelve years old. In Jewish tradition, a boy is considered a man at age twelve.
- v. 43: Mary and Joseph were unaware that Jesus had stayed behind in Jerusalem. Evidently, Jesus did not deem it necessary to confer with his parents on this decision.
- v. 44: Mary and Joseph assumed that Jesus was in the company of the people who had journeyed to Jerusalem with their family. Obviously, even the parents of Jesus were capable of making wrong assumptions.

v. 45: Mary and Joseph looked everywhere for Jesus, but could not find him. They then went back to Jerusalem to try to locate their son.
v. 46: After three days of not knowing the whereabouts of Jesus, they finally found him in the temple, sitting among the teachers, asking and listening to questions.
v.47: Even at the young age of twelve, Jesus' insight and understanding of the Scriptures amazed the teachers of his day.
v. 48: When Mary and Joseph did find their son, they were astonished. They appeared somewhat put out with him or, at the very least, confused by his unusual behavior. Perhaps this was the first time Jesus had chosen a path different from that of his parents. Mary and Joseph were accustomed to a compliant, obedient child, but now they were forced to deal with a misunderstanding that must have appeared quite out of character for Jesus. Their perfect child had confused them, and Mary says to Jesus, "Son, why have you treated us like this? Your father and I have been anxiously searching for you."
v. 49: "Why were you searching for me? Didn't you know I had to be in my Father's house?" Jesus' reply was intended to be neither coy nor haughty. He simply answered his mother's question with one of his own. "Didn't you know I had to be in my Father's house?"

* * * * *

"Mother, *why didn't you know?*" I'm hearing a tone of "You, of all people, should know I had to be in my Father's house." Had to. The implication was that Mary should have or could have known the whereabouts of her son. Perhaps that's why Jesus didn't tell his parents he was staying behind in Jerusalem. Whatever his reason, Jesus obeyed God at the risk of being misunderstood by two godly parents.

Here is the core of the adult child's predicament as it pertains to honoring his/her parents: we're children of our parents, but we're first and foremost children of God, created to fulfill God-given destinies placed in our hearts before we were even born. Our days are numbered and ordained by God. God created us with a purpose and he placed in each of us an internal compass to direct us toward that purpose. Jesus was no different. On that fateful day in Jerusalem, Jesus heard a voice telling him to remain in Jerusalem. Mary and Joseph, on the other hand, had no idea where to look for their son. The bottom line is: Mary and Joseph didn't always hear the voice their son heard. Jesus seemed to naturally know where he was suppose to be on that eventful day in Jerusalem, while it took much effort and an extensive search for Mary and Joseph to locate their child.

To some it might appear Jesus was disobedient—even uncaring—in not telling his parents he was staying in Jerusalem. We know, however, that the opposite was true. Jesus was functioning in perfect obedience to the voice of his heavenly Father, a voice which had, in actuality, greater authority than that even of his parents.

The commandment to "Honor your father and your mother" would be easier to obey if all parents were perfect, always listening to the voice of God and always hearing his will in every situation. We know that's not the case. Our parents are human—*we're human*—and, like Mary and Joseph, we'll "miss it" from time to time. This is precisely the reason we need to be able to hear God's voice for ourselves and to teach our children to do the same.

Note that Instead of feeling threatened when Jesus veered from a family tradition, Mary made a choice. She pondered her son's decision, and, after much consideration, Mary chose to treasure in her heart the fact that Jesus was hearing the voice of his heavenly Father.

One can imagine Mary reliving that particular journey to Jerusalem when her young son took this step into manhood. He was becoming his own person. It would seem Jesus felt confident in his parent's unconditional love for him as he ventured toward spiritual maturity. How encouraging for Jesus to have the support of his earthly parents as he began his walk of faith toward such a compelling destiny.

What makes Jesus' questions—"Why were you searching for me? Didn't you know I had to be in my Father's house?"—so important? Could it be that God never led Mary and Joseph to tell their son of his immaculate conception? Is it possible God wanted Jesus to discover *for himself* that he was the Son of God? His words to Mary on that particular day have a ring of, "Mother, I'm beginning to understand who I am."

GROWING UP

Twelve-year-old Jesus exercised his free will in order to follow the perfect will of his Father. Though his decision was unpopular with his parents, Jesus chose to walk the road true to his person.

It takes a brave person to follow the Lord, especially when allegiance demands that you go against family tradition (as was the case when Jesus stayed behind in Jerusalem). But Jesus would not put tradition above obedience. It seemed nothing would interfere with his flint-like determination to do the will of his Father, not even the threat of being misunderstood by his parents.

Little is said of Jesus' life between the age of twelve, when he stayed behind in Jerusalem, until the time he and his parents attended a wedding at Cana. There is, however, a significant passage which offers us a glimpse into these unrecorded years. We've seen this verse before but it needs repeating.

Then He went down with them and came to Nazareth,
and was subject to them.
Luke 2:51a (NKJV; emphasis mine)

Though Jesus was the only Son of God, he certainly wasn't an only child in the household of Mary and Joseph. Yet, and while living alongside his siblings, Jesus made the decision to place himself under the authority of his parents. He chose the posture of submission and surrendered to the rules of his parents. How refreshing to envision an adolescent boy living out his teenage years with an attitude of submission. Such wisdom Jesus exhibited, even at the tender age of twelve.

And Jesus grew in <u>wisdom</u> and <u>stature</u>,
and in <u>favor</u> with God and men.
Luke 2:52

<u>Wisdom</u>: Greek, *sophia* (sof-ee′-ah): insight into the true nature of things (Vine, 678); wise in a general sense
<u>Stature</u>: Greek, *helikos* (hay-lee′-kos): maturity in years or size; big, great
<u>Favor</u>: Greek, *charis* (khar′-ece): calmly happy or well off; graciousness of manner

SET MY CHILDREN FREE

Into his young adulthood, Jesus followed the voice of his heavenly Father, regardless of whether his parents understood him or not. Mary and Joseph gave their son freedom to choose heavenward. In truth, it would have been a futile attempt to do otherwise.

As parents of adult children, are we willing to give our children the same "freedom to find God" that Mary and Joseph gave Jesus? We must let go of our adult child and avoid the temptation to manipulate him or her toward dependence upon us. We must especially be aware of any disapproval (be it ever so subtle) we'd be tempted to express when our child makes a decision that leads him or her away from home—away from us.

Mary and Joseph were blessed that their son made choices which reflected God's will for his life. Bear in mind, however, these parents were human, and couldn't always have been certain of Jesus' decision-making abilities. Surely there were many times when Mary was found shaking her head, pondering her son's actions, leaning on faith and then remembering the words:

He will be great and will be called the Son of the Most High.
The Lord God will give him the throne of his father David,
and he will reign over the house of Jacob forever; his kingdom will never end.
Luke 1:32–33

Have you ever thought about the life of Jesus from his mother's perspective? Ever wonder if Mary was tempted to influence Jesus' life in such a way as to justify his conception and demonstrate his destiny? Ever wonder about the bittersweet life Mary must have led, as the years of Jesus' childhood clicked by, each one leading her son closer to a cross? Though Mary had divine insight concerning the conception and big picture purpose for the life of her son, she didn't have all the answers. She wasn't God. Even as the chosen mother of the Son of God, Mary was often left with incomplete answers to normal questions a mother would ask. The mother of Jesus—even this mother had to learn to walk by faith.

LETTING GO

Mary watched her son move toward the call of God upon his life. The boy Jesus has grown into manhood when Mary and Jesus are invited to a wedding feast, and it's here at Cana, in the land of Galilee, where Mary seems to have special insight that her son is able to provide.

On the third day a wedding took place at Cana in Galilee.
Jesus' mother was there,
and Jesus and his disciples had also been invited to the wedding.
When the wine was gone, Jesus' mother said to him.
"They have no more wine."
"Woman, why do you involve me?" Jesus replied.
"My hour has not yet come."
His mother said to the servants,
"Do whatever he tells you."
John 2:1-5 (emphasis mine)

I believe Mary knew Jesus would tell the servants to fill the jars with water.

Jesus said to the servants,
"Fill the jars with water": so they filled them to the brim.
Then he told them, "Now draw some out and take it to the master of the banquet."
They did so, and the master of the banquet tasted the water that had been turned into wine. . . This, the first of his miraculous signs Jesus performed in Cana in Galilee.
He thus revealed his glory and his disciples put their faith in him.
John 2:8-9a, 11

There's an exchange of some sort taking place in these passages. Mary tells her son there's a need. Jesus responds that his hour has not yet come. He knows it's coming, the time when his glory will first be revealed, but doesn't acknowledge now is that time. Mary, in spite of her son's hesitancy, suggests Jesus will take action pertaining to the need for more wine. She tells the servants,

"Do whatever he tells you."

Let's take the time to feel the heart of a woman who, when told the Holy Spirit would overshadow her and she would bear the Son of God, showed no hesitation in her attitude of humility and obedience. "I am the Lord's servant," Mary answered. "May it be to me as you have said" (Luke 1:38).

Some thirty-plus years later, her son is on the precipice of revealing that he is the Son of God. Mary had kept these things in her heart and pondered the holiness of it all. Now the destiny of her son is forthcoming. It is the beginning of the end, and I believe she knows this only moments before Jesus does.

"They have no more wine."
"Do whatever he tells you."
I feel a faster heartbeat as Mary speaks these words. Now is the time for the truth she has known all his life to be revealed to the public. Her son is the Son of God.

"Dear woman, why do you involve me?" Jesus replied. "My time has not yet come."
His mother said to the servants, "Do whatever he tells you." "This is the first of his miraculous signs Jesus performed in Cana in Galilee. He thus *revealed his glory* and his disciples put their faith in him" (John 2:1-11).

TRAINING IN HUMILITY

"Come to me, all you who labor and are heavy laden,
and I will give you rest.
Take my yoke upon you and learn from Me,
for I am gentle and lowly in heart,
and you will find rest for your souls."
Matthew 11:28–29 (NKJV)

Meek: Greek, *praos* (prah'-os): gentle, humble, meek, mild
Lowly: Greek, *tapeinos* (tap-i-nos'): depressed, humiliated in circumstances or disposition, cast down, of low degree

Jesus described himself as a gentle man, humble and of low degree. Jesus fulfilled the command to honor his parents with a posture of humility.

Train a child in the way he should go,
and when he is old he will not depart from it.
Proverbs 22:6 (NKJV)

Train: Hebrew, *chanak* (khaw-nak'): to direct, to dedicate, to discipline

Webster's Dictionary lists no fewer than twenty-five definitions to describe the word "train." Within this list are two definitions we need to consider as it relates to training our children to honor their parents.

- Train: to discipline and instruct (as an animal) in the performance of tasks or tricks.
- Train: to treat or manipulate so as to bring some desired form, position, or direction.

In order to be rewarded with a treat, a dog can be trained to perform for its master (come, sit, stay, heel). But we don't want children as pets, and we certainly don't want our children to obey us on the basis of receiving a reward. That's not parenting–it's manipulation. So before we ask our children to obey, we should consider the following:

- our *motives* for requesting obedience, and
- the *means* by which obedience is accomplished.

Children learn most of their values by observing what's valuable to their parents. So, whether we're traveling via the dusty roads out of Egypt or the busy highways of today, whether we want it to be true or otherwise, we can't escape the reality that our children are being trained by the lifestyles they see us living. Are our children observing us honoring God? When Mama and Daddy submit to their Heavenly Father, children see that. And they see when we don't. The most effective means of training our children to honor their parents is to see their parents honoring God.

FAITH-FILLED PARENTING

Here is a trustworthy saying:
If anyone sets his heart on being an overseer, he desires a noble task.
Now the overseer must be above reproach, the husband of but one wife, temperate,
self-controlled, respectable, hospitable, able to teach, not given to drunkenness,
not violent but gentle, not quarrelsome, not a lover of money.
He must manage his own family well
and see that his children obey him with proper respect.
(If anyone does not know how to manage his own family,
how can he take care of God's church?)
I Timothy 3:1–5 (emphasis mine)

Abraham will surely become a great and powerful nation,
and all nations on earth will be blessed through him.
For I have chosen him,
so that he will direct his children and his household after him
to keep the way of the Lord
by doing what is right and just,
so that the Lord will bring about for Abraham what he has promised him.
Genesis 18:18–19 (emphasis mine)

God blesses men who direct their children in the ways of God. God released his promises to Abraham because Abraham taught his children what is right and just.

Looking closer into the character of Abraham:

Abram obeyed God, even when it meant leaving his country.

The Lord said to Abram, "Leave your country, your people and your father's household
and go to the land I will show you. So Abram left, as the Lord had told him.
Genesis 12:1, 4a

Abram was generous. He gave his brother, Lot, first choice of land.

Is not the whole land before you? Let's part company.
It you go to the left, I'll go to the right; if you go to the right, I'll go to the left.
Genesis 13:9

Abram was courageous.

When Abram heard that his relative had been taken captive, he called out the 318 trained men born in his household and went in pursuit as far as Dan. During the night Abram divided his men to attack them and he routed them, pursuing them as far as Hobah, north of Damascus.
He recovered all the goods and
brought back his relative Lot and his possessions,
together with the women and the other people.
Genesis 14:14–16

Being willing to follow God, demonstrating generosity, exhibiting faith in God, proving himself a valiant warrior, all highlight the noble character of Abraham. But it would be much later in life, as a parent of a special son named Isaac, when Abraham's character would be put to the supreme test.

Some time later God tested Abraham.
He said to him, "Abraham!" "Here I am," he replied. Then God said,
"Take your son, your only son Isaac, whom you love,
and go to the region of Moriah.
Sacrifice him there as a burnt offering
on one of the mountains I will tell you about.
Genesis 22:1–2

Abraham obeyed.

Abraham took the wood of the burnt offering and placed it on his son Isaac,
and he himself carried the fire and the knife.
As the two of them went on together,
Isaac spoke up and said to his father Abraham,
"Father?" "Yes, my son?" Abraham replied.
"The fire and the wood are here, but where is the lamb for a burnt offering?"
Genesis 22:6–7

Can you hear the absolute trust Isaac has for his father? Scripture offers *not a hint* of resistance from Isaac. It seems obvious Isaac intends to obey his father. However, if you didn't know the events of this fateful day, you could easily anticipate *Abraham* would grow fearful, become weak, even faint at the thought of carrying out the instructions of his Lord.

Here come perhaps the most faith-filled words ever spoken by a parent.

Abraham answered,
"God will provide for himself the lamb for a burnt offering, my son."
Genesis 22:8a

When he reached the place God had told him about,
Abraham built an altar there and arranged the wood on it.
He bound his son Isaac and laid him on the altar on top of the wood.
Then he reached out his hand and took the knife to slay his son.
Genesis 22:9–10

But the angel of the Lord called out to him from heaven, "Abraham! Abraham!"
"Here I am," he replied. "Do not lay a hand on the boy," he said.
"Do not do anything to him. Now I know that you fear God,
<u>because you have not withheld from me your son, your only son</u>.
Abraham looked up and there in a thicket he saw a ram caught by its horns.
He went over and took the ram and sacrificed it as a burnt offering instead of his son.
So Abraham called that place The Lord Will Provide. And to this day it is said,
"On the mountain of the Lord it will be provided."
Genesis 22:11–14 (emphasis mine)

Placing God above all others, withholding nothing from God, not even his beloved, only son Isaac: this is how Abraham proved his love for God.

And this is how God proved his love for us.

"For God so loved the world that he gave his one and only son,
that whoever believes in him shall not perish but have eternal life."
John 3:16

It would be wise to pause and examine our personal commitment to "Honor our Parent." Abraham was willing for his son to suffer in order that he, the parent, obey his heavenly Father. Mercifully, God didn't require the life of young Isaac, but he could have. Regardless of God's intervention, Abraham proved his love by being willing to obey God at any cost, even if it meant the suffering of his own son.

Abraham honored Jehovah by having no other gods before him, not even his own child. When we become parents, the question is this: "Are we able to hold out, can we bear through until we've obeyed the Lord in all things, in particular the training of our children?" When our child begins to complain, will we bow to his whimpers, or will we rise to the life of obedience to which God has called *us*?

Isaac was blessed to have a father who loved God above all else and who obeyed God at any cost. Isaac saw his father honor his Father. Children's eyes see a lot.

FEAR OR FAITH

Chapter 27 of Genesis tells the story of Isaac's wife, Rebekah, a once beautiful, generous, hospitable bride, who was now a mother filled with fear and insecurities. The story goes on to say that she even stooped so low as to eavesdrop on a conversation between her husband and his favored son, Esau. Then, taking advantage of her aging husband's blindness, Rebekah contrived a plan that would cause her favored son, Jacob, to receive the blessing of the firstborn child, a blessing that rightfully belonged to Esau.

Rebekah got her way—but in getting what she wanted Jacob was forced to move to another land, thus separating her from the child she dearly loved. It's quite possible that Rebekah regretted her decision to become involved in the fate of the firstborn blessing. Perhaps God had a better plan, one that would allow the blessing to be given to Jacob while also allowing him to remain close to his family.

This propensity to deceive is evident in Rebekah, in her son Jacob, and in the generations that followed. Read Chapter 34 of Genesis and see how the deceptive behavior of the sons of Jacob (Rebekah's grandchildren) brought trouble to their family. Read Genesis, Chapter 34 to learn about the deceptive way Jacob's sons dealt with the Shechemites, resulting in a loss of trust between Jacob and his neighboring tribes.

FAITHFUL PARENTING

Rebekah is not unlike many of today's parents. It's natural to believe Rebekah had high hopes for the lives of both her sons. But as the life of Jacob began to take an unexpected turn, something took hold of this mother. Rebekah that feared God's word—" . . . and the older would serve the younger"—would not come to pass unless *she* helped it along (Genesis 25:23b). Fear spoke to Rebekah and said something like this: "Rebekah, I give you *permission to deceive* in order to control your family in the way of the Lord." How sad for Rebekah (and her family) that she believed God needed deception in order to accomplish his promises.

Notice the contrast between Abraham's style of parenting and that of Rebekah. Rebekah held tightly to her son, while Abraham was willing to let go of his. Mary, the mother of Jesus, is another parent who is equally worthy of our respect. Like Abraham, Mary was a parent who fully trusted her Heavenly Father to take care of her son.

We have the same choice to make as these parents. We can follow the parental path of Rebekah and teach our children to obey us, even when our counsel is self-serving, deceptive, controlling—even when it defrauds our fellow man and dishonors our heavenly Father. We can exert that kind of control over our children. Or we can parent like Abraham and Mary: confident in God's character, knowing his ways so well that we rest in the understanding that *God can be trusted, even with the people we love most.*

What kind of parents parented you? Were they filled more with fear or with faith? Were you reared in a Christian home? Did your parents teach you to love God and his commandments? Perhaps your physical needs were met, but no one opened God's Word to share its life-giving gems with you. Perhaps you've come to love God in spite of your childhood.

Whoever you are, whatever your past, God wants to make something beautiful out of your life. God is able to make everything come together and be called good (Romans 8:28).

A Mother's Prayer

by Pat Menser

I'm sorry for the years gone by, the days so long ago.
They should be full of happy thoughts, instead they bring us woe.
How I wish that I could call them back and do it all again.
I'd change so very many things that now I see as sin.

I'd hold you in my arms and say how much you mean to me.
I'd gladly welcome every call of "Mama, come and see!"
I'd push aside the dishes, tell the work that it can wait.
My daughter has a need right now for which I won't be late.

Her heart was young and tender—as I looked into her eyes,
I knew that she'd depend on me to comfort all her cries.
But I turned my heart toward the world, away from child and home.
Bewildered, lonely, young and lost, I've lived my life alone.

Now, daughter, please accept these words, though late as they may be,
As my thoughts brought to you through Him to comfort and appease.
For years have hardened self and pride and make it hard to say
That I love you just the way you are—since then and still today.

I'm sorry for my failures and the words I couldn't speak.
I'm sorry for the nights I left you comfortless and weak.
I'm sorry for the times I put myself above your needs.
Just know that I have lived with guilt from which I must be freed.

That's why I'm praying now, "*Lord, take these hurts of hers and mine,*
Bury them, dear Lord I pray, and never to remind
me of the past that tries to haunt me, of the years I strayed away.
And help my child to know she's loved on my "forgiveness day.""

After studying the commandment to "Honor Your Parents," perhaps you've come to more fully appreciate the blessing of parents who loved the Lord. That may not be the case. Maybe you relate more to the child who wrote this poem, or perhaps the mother who is in search of forgiveness? You may be led to pray for someone who is struggling with fear and the challenges of being a parent. You may want to pray for one of your parents. *You may want to pray for yourself.*

Honoring Parents

PRINCIPLES

1. God places a divine destiny and the desire to fulfill that destiny within each of us.
2. We must be able to hear God's voice and teach our children to do the same.
3. Children are trained by observing the lifestyles of their parents.
4. There are times when, in order to follow God's will for our lives, we must break with family tradition.
5. Abraham was a faithful parent, causing him to trust God with his son.
6. Rebekah was a fearful parent who tried to manipulate the lives of her children.
7. Jesus obeyed his Father without grumbling.
8. It takes humility to honor our parents.
9. It takes faith to honor our parents.
10. A humble person is beautiful and precious in the sight of God.
11. God gives grace to the humble and will lift him up at the right time.
12. There are benefits in honoring our parents.
13. We can forgive our parents and learn from their mistakes.

Honoring Parents

DISCUSSION QUESTIONS

1. Can you Identify a time when you obeyed God but were misunderstood by your parents?
2. How did you feel then about being misunderstood?
3. How do you feel now about being misunderstood?
4. At the wedding of Cana, what do you make of the exchange between Jesus and his mother, and then Mary and the servants? If you're a parent, try to relate this scene to your own experiences.
5. What are some specific ways you can teach your children to grow in wisdom and in favor with God and men?
6. In your own words, paraphrase how Jesus' parents felt when he told them the reason he stayed behind in Jerusalem (Luke 2:50).
7. Put yourself in Mary's place when Jesus stayed behind in Jerusalem without consulting her (Luke 2:51b). How might you respond in a similar situation with your own child?
8. Compare "honoring" your parents with being "subject" to your parents.
9. Why do you think the benefit of a long and enjoyable life is related to the command to honor your father and your mother?
10. What are some consequences a child might endure if he makes choices which do not honor his parents?
11. How is it that a parent's motives for wanting obedience become misguided?
12. Is there a specific action you can take which would show honor to your parents, even if they are deceased?

Anyone who hates his brother is a murderer,
and you know that no murderer has eternal life in him.

1 John 3:15

Chapter 6

Do Not Murder

Exodus 20:13

"Give God Your Grudges."

In this chapter you will read about . . .

- the reasons behind Esau's murderous heart toward his brother, Jacob;
- the highest purpose of God's goodness;
- the role of repentance in healing a murderous heart;
- the Biblical protocol for dealing with a person who has sinned against you;
- the proper response toward a repentant brother/sister in Christ.

Hebrew/Greek word studies: goodness, repentance, forgive, compassion, kill/murder

The desire to murder is rooted in the soil of offense. Therefore, to deal with a murderous heart, we must address the issue of forgiving those who have offended us. The goal of this chapter is to demonstrate that forgiveness is best achieved when our attention is focused on the goodness of God in our lives, *remembering that we are sinners in need of forgiveness* and then (by God's Spirit living within us) offering our forgiveness to others. Scripture demands that we give our wrath to God, look for the good in others, pray for our enemies, and anticipate a celebration of restored fellowship.

And though it may seem impossible to forgive others for the pain they've brought into our lives, if we truly believe the Scriptures, then we're forced to acknowledge that through Christ all things are possible. Nothing is excluded in the phrase "all things." Therefore, through Christ we *can* do all things, which includes the ability to forgive.

"You have heard that it was said to the people long ago,
'Do not murder,
and anyone who murders will be subject to judgment.'
But I tell you that anyone who is angry with his brother will be subject to judgment."
Anyone who hates his brother is a murderer,
and you know that no murderer has eternal life in him.
Matthew 5:21, 1 John 3:15

It's time to return to Esau. We'll remember Esau as the son who was deceived by his mother, Rebekah, and defrauded by his brother, Jacob. Join with me as we use our God-given imaginations to hear what a conversation with Esau might reveal. Maybe there's more we can learn from the life of Esau.

"Esau, would you mind some company?"

"If you'd like," he answered.

"I'd like to hear your side of the story."

Silence was his only response.

"Let me rephrase. . . I'd be honored to hear how you felt when you were deceived by your brother."

"It was also my mother," he reminded me.

"Yes, I'm aware of her part in the deception. Would you like to talk about it?"

"It's difficult to put into words," he explained.

"Esau, perhaps it would help you to share your story if you knew there were others who could learn from your experience."

Softly he spoke. "I'm called 'the hairy one' and 'the hunter.' "

"Yes, Scripture says you are a skillful hunter—a man of the field."

"I like to eat," he confessed.

"Yes, go on."

Dropping his head, Esau muttered, "I was promiscuous in my youth. Some even called me a whoremonger."

Now it was I who was silent, sensing that Esau was ready to release his emotions.

Sobbing, Esau said, "Why do people only remember the bad in me? I'm more than the heathen, wicked man you read about. In truth, it was never my blood that was chosen to flow through the veins of the Messiah.

And though I was not the chosen, I was called of God to father the Edomites. God never forgot me. I suppose, however, that compared to Jehovah's love for Jacob, his love for me appeared as hatred."

"Esau, what have you learned from all this? What is your message to the people?"

"How can I make you understand?" Esau asked. "Is there a man left who's not been deceived by Jacob?"

"Esau, you're confusing me. Please be more specific. I want to hear *your* side of the story," I pleaded.

"It's always been a struggle between Jacob and me. Mother used to speak of days when her womb was alive with activity. But Jacob and I were never identical in physical appearance and certainly not in temperament. Jacob was the quiet homebody while I enjoyed the outdoors.

"I'm blessed to say that Father's love for me was great. There is, however, nothing like the love of a mother, and that's one of the many things in life that eluded me. I always knew Mother favored Jacob. Children know these things.

"The day I lost my birthright was the beginning of my demise."

Once when Jacob was cooking some stew,
Esau came in from the open country, famished.
He said to Jacob, "Quick, let me have some of that red stew! I'm famished!"
(That is why he was also called Edom.)
Jacob replied, "First sell me your birthright."
"Look, I am about to die," Esau said. "What good is the birthright to me?"
But Jacob said, "Swear to me first."
So he swore an oath to him, selling his birthright to Jacob.
Then Jacob gave Esau some bread and some lentil stew.
He ate and drank, and then got up and left. So Esau despised his birthright.
Genesis 25:29–34

"I was hungry. I was fooled and not thinking straight. So I gave it away. My most important possession—my birthright—I gave away. It was an asinine thing to do. For the longest time I couldn't think about that day without feeling hatred for my brother, for God, and, I guess, especially for myself. There were days I didn't know who I hated most.

"Then came my day of bitterness. Father was old. Age had dimmed his vision. He didn't know how much longer he had to live and so he asked that I go to the field and kill some venison and make him the savory food he loved so much. I was quick to obey.

"It was while I was in the field, obeying the will of my father, when Jacob used my name and Father's deep love for Jehovah in order to trick our ailing father. It was a loathsome thing to do."

Jacob said to his father, "I am Esau your firstborn. I have done as you told me.
Please sit up and eat some of my game so that you may give me your blessing."
Isaac asked his son, "How did you find it so quickly, my son?"
"The Lord your God gave me success," he replied.
Genesis 27:19–20

Esau continued.

"Jacob is a liar. God didn't give him success. He deceived Father—taking advantage of his age and poor eyesight. How could anyone stoop so low? I'll take the blame for giving away my birthright in exchange for that bowl of wretched soup, but being tricked by your own brother in order to receive the blessing of the firstborn . . . well, how would that make you feel?"

"How did that make you feel?" I asked.

"Cheated. Stolen from. He's a thief too, you know. He stole my clothes and wore them so he would smell like me. And even to this day many don't remember that Jacob betrayed his own father with a kiss."

Then his father Isaac said to him, "Come here, my son, and kiss me."
So he went to him and kissed him.
When Isaac caught the smell of his clothes, he blessed him . . .
Genesis 27:26–27a

ESAU: THE OFFENDED

"I remember Father trembling when he realized he'd given my blessing to another. With many tears I sought for the blessing of the firstborn to return to me, but it was not to be."

Gently I asked, "Esau, how did you manage to go on? The shame of giving away your birthright for a bowl of soup and the betrayal of your mother and brother—how did you handle such pain?"

"At first I could think of nothing but murder. I purposed in my heart that when Father passed away and the days of his mourning were over, I'd kill that son of deception."

"But you didn't do it, Esau. You didn't murder Jacob. In fact, if you don't mind me saying, you eventually forgave him. This is what we want to understand. Please, Esau, please tell us how you were able to forgive your brother."

Lifting his head Esau looked into my eyes and said, "*That* is the story I've longed to tell."

* * * * *

Forgiveness. That's the untold story of Esau. Yes, we're quick to remember Esau's shady reputation, his failures and his faults, but today we're pursuing the good side of Esau, the part of Esau which was able to run and embrace a brother who, years earlier, had defrauded him and brought such grief into Esau's life that murdering his brother seemed to be the likely outcome of their relationship.

But in order to see the good side of Esau, we're forced to turn our attention to the not so good side of Esau's younger brother, Jacob. Jacob was the homebody of the family and the son whom Rebekah favored. Jacob was the son who deceived both his father and his brother, and, as a result of Jacob's deception, Esau held a heavy grudge against his brother, even planning to murder Jacob once their father had died. Rebekah heard of Esau's ill will toward his brother and encouraged Jacob to leave their home in order to put some distance between these two siblings.

JACOB: THE OFFENDER

Jacob had clearly offended his brother. Years passed. Jacob was guilty, and the thought of seeing Esau caused him great distress.

Jacob sent messengers ahead of him to his brother Esau in the land of Seir,
the country of Edom. He instructed them:
"This is what you are to say to my master Esau:
'Your servant Jacob says,
I have been staying with Laban and have remained there till now.
I have cattle and donkeys, sheep and goats, menservants and maidservants.
Now I am sending this message to my lord, that I may find favor in your eyes.' ". . .
In great fear and distress Jacob divided the people
who were with him into two groups,
the flocks and herds and camels as well. He thought,
"If Esau comes and attacks one group, the group that is left may escape."
Genesis 32:3–8 (emphasis mine)

Then Jacob prayed, "O God of my father Abraham,
God of my father Isaac, O Lord, who said to me,
'Go back to your country and your relatives, and I will make you prosper,'
I am unworthy of all the kindness and faithfulness you have shown your servant.
I had only my staff when I crossed the Jordan, but now I have become two groups.
Save me, I pray, from the hand of my brother Esau, for I am afraid he will come
and attack me, and also the mothers with their children.. . .
He (Jacob) selected a gift for this brother Esau:
two hundred female goats and twenty male goats,
two hundred ewes and twenty rams,
thirty female camels with their young . . .
He instructed the one in the lead: "When my brother Esau meets you and asks,
'To whom do you belong, where are you going, and who owns all these animals in
front of you?' then you are to say, 'They belong to your servant Jacob.
They are a gift sent to my lord Esau, and he is coming behind us.' "
Genesis 32:9–10, 17–18 (emphasis mine)

Jacob has had a big-time change in his attitude toward Esau. He's humbled to the point of being afraid, wanting to appease his brother's wrath by bringing him gifts. Jacob considers Esau to be his lord and Jacob to be Esau's servant.

It's now the day before Jacob would see Esau. He's on the precipice of an encounter with a person he has deeply offended. Nightfall is approaching.

So Jacob was left alone, and a man wrestled with him till daybreak.
When the man saw that he could not overpower him,
he touched the socket of Jacob's hip so that his hip was wrenched
as he wrestled with the man. Then the man said, "Let me go, for it is daybreak."
But Jacob replied, "I will not let you go unless you bless me."
Then man asked him, "What is your name?" "Jacob," he answered.
Then the man said, "Your name will no longer be Jacob, but Israel,
because you have struggled with God and with men and have overcome."
Jacob said, "Please tell me your name." But he replied, "Why do you ask my name?"
Then he blessed him there.
Genesis 32:24–29

On this momentous evening, Jacob the Deceiver is in a wrestling match, determined to legitimately receive the blessing that he had illegitimately taken from Esau. And he wins the match. Jacob struggles with God and with men and he comes out on top. Even his name is changed.

Your name will no longer be Jacob, but Israel. It appears more was changed than Jacob's—excuse me, "Israel's"—name: Israel's blessing was no longer a stolen one. It didn't come by trickery or deception; it came from God. Though still uncertain of Esau's response to him, Israel (now carrying the legitimate blessing of God upon his life) walks humbly toward Esau and bows to the ground as he approaches his brother. Feel free to personally embrace the following verse.

But Esau ran to meet Jacob and embraced him;
he threw his arms around his neck and kissed him.
And they wept.
Genesis 33:4

What a welcome! What a sweet, heartfelt welcome. Here we see that Jacob isn't the only brother with a changed attitude. Notice how Esau has progressed from planning the murder of his brother to throwing his arms around Jacob and crying as he kissed him.

But how did forgiveness win in the "battle of bitterness" waged between these two brothers? First, we see the offender *getting honest with himself and with God.* It was a struggle, but Jacob was willing to do whatever it took to set things right with God and receive God's blessing upon his life. Next, Jacob purposed in his heart to *make restitution* for that which he had stolen from his brother. In hopes of gaining Esau's favor, Jacob offered Esau many gifts (goats, ewes, rams, camels, cows, bulls and donkeys). Listen carefully to Esau's gracious response to these gifts.

Esau asked, "What do you mean by all these droves I met?"
"To find favor in your eyes, my lord," he said.
But Esau said, "I already have plenty, my brother. Keep what you have for yourself."
And because Jacob insisted, Esau accepted it.
Genesis 33:8–9, 11b

Enough/Plenty: Hebrew, *rab* (rab): abundant in quantity, size, age, number, rank and quality; abound; exceedingly, full, great, very much, plenteous; multiply; ten thousands

Esau had plenty. Jacob's offense hadn't robbed Esau of a prosperous life. Esau recognized God's provision in the midst of his brother's offense. And let's not forget that Esau was an unwitting cohort in Jacob's scheme to attain Esau's blessing *and his birthright*. Esau thought little enough of his birthright to sell it for a bowl of soup. And though Esau's past was riddled with mistakes, poor judgment, rejection, deception, loss–all of which resulted in a vengeful and murderous heart–it was God's love, God's provision, *God's plenty* that healed Esau of his past wounds, enabled him to forgive Jacob and then reestablished a relationship that had been severely (nearly mortally) wounded. God is the Person who deserves full credit for two brothers, seemingly estranged for life, being reconciled and, years later, able to come together in order to bury their beloved father, Isaac.

Then he breathed his last and died and was gathered to his people,
old and full of years.
And his sons Esau and Jacob buried him.
Genesis 35:29

THE GOODNESS OF GOD

And he said,
"I have plenty, my brother;
let what you have be your own."
Genesis 33:9

Plenty: God had been generous with Esau. He'd given Esau more than enough—great, full abounding in number, quality and quantity. God's kindness provided Esau with the ability to forgive his brother. God's kindness allowed Jacob and Esau, together, to bury their father, Isaac. But the deeper motive for God's goodness was to bring Esau, as well as us, to a much richer destination.

Or do you show contempt for the riches of his kindness, tolerance and patience,
not realizing that God's kindness leads you toward repentance?
Romans 2:4

Kindness/Goodness: Greek, *chrestotes* (khrase-tos'): usefulness, kindness; to furnish what is needed
Repentance: Greek, *metanoeo* (met-an-o-eh'-o): to think differently, to reform, to reconsider, to reverse

Perhaps you're feeling as Esau felt when life defrauded him. Do you feel robbed of what is rightfully yours? Have you been cheated by a business partner? Does your mother favor another child? Even worse, are you angry with yourself for choices you've made which have contributed to your present predicament?

Then maybe a good place to begin is to allow God's goodness to lead you to repentance. Take responsibility for selling your birthright for a bowl of soup. Repent of your past, reconcile with those whom you've offended and who've offended you, and then forgive yourself for your personal failures. Like Esau, you may have given away your birthright for a temporarily-satisfying-bowl-of-soup. If so, please remember the rest of Esau's story. God had plenty of blessings still ahead for Esau and, *when true repentance is present*, God is eager to show his goodness and to give you plenty.

Beware, however, of our inclination to mistake God's goodness as evidence of condoning our sin. This is a terrible misuse of mercy, often called "cheap grace." God's goodness is not meant to condone our sin or to lead us into deeper sin; God's kindness is meant to lead us to repentance.

So are you sorry you sinned? Sorry, that's not enough. Worldly sorrow is merely a sadness that your sin was found out, that it caused pain to others, and that the consequences are difficult to endure. Worldly sorrow focuses on self and the personal discomfort of bad decisions. This type of sorrow is deceptive in that it causes us to stop short of true repentance. God wants his goodness to take us to its divine destination: past the valley of regret . . . through the tunnel of remorse . . . until we arrive at the place of *godly* sorrow.

Godly sorrow brings repentance that leads to salvation and leaves no regret, but worldly sorrow brings death. See what this godly sorrow has produced in you: what earnestness, what eagerness to clear yourselves, what indignation, what alarm, what longing, what concern, what readiness to see justice done.
2 Corinthians 7:10-11a

Let's continue on our journey. How is it exactly that God's kindness leads us to repentance? Consider this: when we sin, we know it. We know when our behavior is an affront to God. We know we don't deserve his goodness; we deserve punishment. God's kindness has opened our eyes to see our sin from his point of view, and we're saddened that our behavior doesn't reflect the God whom we claim to serve. Then, when God loves us in spite of our failures and offers mercy instead of deserved judgment, we hardly know how to respond to such kindness, such tolerance and patience. How can we resist this love? Eventually the force of God's love causes us to think differently about our sin, and we want to reform our behavior to conform to the love God has shown us. Now we're experiencing godly sorrow.

"Esau, you've taught us many things. It's encouraging to know you forgave Jacob for the pain he caused you. Your life shows that often the greatest source of our pain is either our own choices or the choices of a family member. But the most important lesson you taught us, Esau, is that *recognizing God's goodness towards us is what enables us to forgive others.* Thanks for that reminder, Esau."

"Thanks for listening."

FORGIVE

It's difficult to forgive. Without God's help it seems almost impossible to lift the heavy weight of life's injustices and lay it aside. But if deeds done against us aren't put away, they tend to become stumbling blocks in our lives, obstructing the pathway God has chosen for us to follow.

Let's continue the study of the sixth commandment, "You shall not murder," by taking a preventive posture. As we've studied earlier, murder has its roots in the soil of unforgiveness.

And when you stand praying,
if you hold anything against anyone, forgive him,
so that your Father in heaven may forgive you your sins.
Mark 11:25

Forgive: Greek, *aphiemi* (af-ee'-ay-mee): to forsake, to lay aside, to yield up

Years ago I stitched a needlepoint sampler with a small, red-and-brown brick house in the middle, surrounded by hearts. The sampler reads:

A house is made of brick and stone.
A home is made of love alone.

Forgiveness reminds me of an interior designer whose job is to soften our hearts with the gracious nature of God's love. Forgiveness is the kind of decorator who's adamant about wanting our homes rid of rigid or bitter furnishings. One of the first decorating tips Forgiveness gives is that we make the deliberate, determined choice to *look for the good* in the very things we've grown to dislike—things which in the past have caused us grief and discontent. Forgiveness will insist we let go of old, worn out offenses and replace them with new, fresh and free "pillows of pardon."

"Looking for the good" in the people God has put in our lives is the most tasteful decorating decision we can make. Why is this so? Because when forgiveness convinces us to look for the good and stop trying to change people, a strange thing begins to happen: we actually begin to accept these people as they are.

Remember that the highest purpose of forgiveness is not to change the character or the opinion of the offender (though God may have some changes in mind). The highest purpose of forgiveness is to change the attitude of the offended. Forgiveness frees the offended person from her mindset of fault-finding, frustration, resentment and revenge to one of gracious acceptance and gratitude.

A few years back there was a TV show called *Trading Spaces*. In this show two neighbors trade homes and redecorate a room in each other's houses. That may work on TV. It might even work in the physical world in general, but it won't work in the spiritual lives of our family and loved ones. We can't go to into the spiritual homes of the people we love and fix what's ailing them. We can't "make it all right." The truth is: it's not our job to clean up their messes. That's between them and God. In the meantime (I know I'm repeating myself), *we do have other work to do.*

Finally, brothers, whatever is true, whatever is noble, whatever is right,
whatever is pure, whatever is lovely, whatever is admirable–
if anything is excellent or praiseworthy–think about such things.
Philippians 4:8

LEAVE ROOM FOR GOD

Do not repay anyone evil for evil.
Be careful to do what is right in the eyes of everybody.
If it is possible, as far as it depends on you, live at peace with everyone.
Do not take revenge, my friends, but leave room for God's wrath:
for it is written: "It is mine to avenge; I will repay," says the Lord.
Romans 12:17–19

Have you ever painted a room with all the furniture still in place? You're constantly bumping into lamps and having to work around chairs and end tables. The job would be much easier if the furniture was either moved to the center of the room or out of the way all together.

I think it's the same way with God. Often we get in God's way when he wants to clean up the wounded rooms of our lives. Without realizing it, we interfere with his business, and he literally has to work around us. The result is that, rather than helping the situation, we inadvertently become an obstacle with which God has to contend.

But it's not easy leaving our **O**ffended/**W**ounded rooms (I'll call them our "**OW**" rooms, since that's where we were hurt). We've been living in these rooms for a long time, likely a lifetime. OW rooms are where we were hurt, offended, bruised and possibly deeply scarred. Sad to say, many of us have grown comfortable living in our OW rooms. We're convinced we belong here, and can't imagine living anywhere else. This is, after all, our personal, private, one-of-a-kind-reserved-exclusively-for-the-wounded-elite room. We know every crook and cranny of our OW room. We've earned the right to live in our room, and we really do believe that if God intends to redecorate our room, he needs our help.

God doesn't need our help. What God really needs is for us to believe he has our best interests in mind and to trust him enough to move aside–get out of the way and allow him liberty to paint healing into our lives in whatever shade he sees fit. Submitting to his will for our rooms usually happens when we become tired enough, sad enough, sick or lonely enough to admit we don't like our OW rooms any more. They're not working for us. They are old and dated and we need help. We may not know just exactly how to be helped, but at least we're looking for a way out of our rooms.

It's OK to not know how God is going to change our room. It's OK to be confused. It's OK to not have all the answers. We are, after all, wounded, lame and most likely limping. Many of us are like Esau: we *have* been mistreated, we *have* been neglected, our parents *have* favored other siblings. We've been hushed and told our opinions don't matter.

They matter, and it's OK to be wounded. But let's also admit it's an overwhelming task to become *un*-wounded and *un*-offended. We really do need help: God's help. We can't get healthy and cleaned up all by ourselves. Lord, have mercy: we're lame and limping people here.

So what *can* we do? Well, if we must do something, let's do this. Let's get out of God's way and allow him carte blanche access to our wounded rooms. Let's admit we've tried to live in our rooms, painted, rearranged and made excuses for our rooms, and they're still ugly. Let's finally and deliberately get out of God's way and allow him complete access to our injustices and unmet needs. Let's see what God can do when we quit giving him advice on how to decorate our rooms. He is, after all, the Professional. And, who knows, when it's all said and done, when we're told to open our spiritual eyes and feast upon our new room, maybe, just maybe, our OW room will become our WOW room!

God knows it takes effort to look for the good. The pure, just, and lovely—even more effort. Yet this is what our Father asks us to do. He's given us the responsibility to pursue peace and, "as far as it depends on us[,] to live at peace with everyone" (Romans 12:18).

I AM THE PARENT

Being a parent of two sons helps me understand the concept of living at peace with others while allowing God to avenge a situation. Many times—did I say many? I meant a whole lot more than *many* . . . all too often, lots of times—I would be in another room in our house, and things would be peaceful, when I'd hear a distinctive hand-to-flesh slap, followed by a loud "Whaaaaaaaaaa!!!" I knew what had happened before I ever arrived at the scene. You remember Little John, don't you? Well, he would routinely annoy and pester his older brother Aaron until Aaron would have enough. That's when Aaron would take it upon himself to discipline little brother. As a parent, I'm now in a frustrating situation. Granted, John was being a brat and deserved to be disciplined, but it's difficult for a compassionate parent (that's me) to inflict more punishment (correct and effective punishment) on a child who is already crying and in pain.

What really happened is that my offended child (that would be Aaron) didn't leave room for the wrath of the person in authority (that would be me). Older brother took it upon himself to discipline *my child*. Big brother hasn't learned that it's not his responsibility to train my child—besides which, he is woefully inadequate as a trainer, being but a child himself.

It helps to remember we're all children of God, equal brothers and sisters in the Lord, but certainly not an equal parent to God. God is the Parent, and he is fully able to deliver justice if we'll get out of his way and "leave room for his wrath." As brothers and sisters in Christ we're accountable to one another, pursuing the holiness of God in our lives and in the lives of fellow believers. And surely God uses fellow believers to guide and deliver truth to one another, but divine discipline ultimately and solely belongs with the Father.

I have written you in my letter not to associate with sexually immoral people—
not at all meaning the people of this world who are immoral,
or the greedy and swindlers, or idolaters.
In that case you would have to leave this world.
But now I am writing you that you must not associate
with anyone who calls himself a brother
but is sexually immoral or greedy, an idolater or a slanderer, a drunkard or
a swindler. With such a man do not even eat.
1 Corinthians 5:9–11 (emphasis mine)

Paul made a clear distinction between people of the world *versus* people who call themselves brothers in Christ.

Perfect Love

by Pat Menser
(*1 John 4:7–18, Psalms:13,1 Corinthians:13*)

Your words are etched with malice,
though you try to hide your hate.
But I can see your hurt within,
I give to thee my grace.

Resentment lurks behind your eyes
and waits to watch me fall.
But it shall find no root in me,
I give my wealth, my all.

Subtly you stick me
with your taunts and sneers and stabs.
I walk away in silent pain,
and give thee tears instead.

You boast of your achievements
and you talk of future schemes.
You never ask what's in my heart.
I give to thee my dreams.

At times your sorrow overflows
and falls upon my sleeve.
It's then I stay close by your side,
and give to thee my peace.

I am devoted to your care,
Yes, loyalty–to you–a must.
Still you betray me yet again?
I give to thee my trust.

I bear, believe, and hope for you
God's blessings from above.
And though you've yet to open it,
I give thee perfect love.

Powerful emotions, love and hate. Only God's grace allows us to love a person who has hurt us deeply. Our flesh will desire its "right to vengeance." Perfect love, God's love, guides us to a place where we're able to absorb wounds inflicted upon us by others. Kyle Matthews writes these lyrics in his song, "Teach Me To Speak Your Language":

"You see true love cannot stand to be mistaken.
It forsakes its own good to be understood."

Perfect love forsakes its own good for the benefit of another. Perfect love is a function of faith in that it's certain God's love, his mercy and, sometimes, even his discipline will prevail.

Throughout the course of our lifetimes we will, no doubt, share the chair of the offended as well as the offender. As much as it hurts to be offended, however, it's sometimes more painful to face the truth that we are the offender.

For those of us who have wounded someone we love, we need to be clear that we can't buy our way back into their graces. In fact, when we recall the story of Esau, we'll remember that Esau didn't ask for an apology from Jacob, nor did he want the gifts Jacob was offering. All Esau really wanted from his relative was a kiss and a hug.

But Esau ran to meet Jacob and embraced him;
he threw his arms around his neck and kissed him.
And they wept.
Genesis 33:4

Are you feeling wounded over the loss of a relationship? Deep down do you wish things were different? Then *perhaps* it's time to consider reconciliation. Think about it: you stand to gain fellowship with someone whose friendship, at one time, meant a lot to you. But before you move forward, make sure you've gone inward to that place where God and you settle this issue. There you will understand that the purpose of approaching the person who has offended you is not so you can forgive him. Why isn't it? Because genuine forgiveness is something you give your offender regardless of whether he asks for it or not. Forgiveness is not based on a person's response to his sin, but on your response to being sinned against. This principle of giving forgiveness before it's ever requested is exemplified most perfectly by our heavenly Father.

But God demonstrated his own love for us in this:
While we were still sinners, Christ died for us.
Romans 5:8

Christ loved us while we were still living in sin, before we were aware of our sin, before we recognized how much our sin hurt him, before we accepted his unconditional love for us, and regardless of how undeserving of or ungrateful for his love we were. Christ demonstrated his love for us *before we knew we needed it.*

With these thoughts in mind, what purpose, then, does it serve to confront the person who has offended us? If we've already forgiven his behavior–love him and want God's best for him–why bring up a past wound or offense? Maybe it's for the sake of the offender. Perhaps our offender needs to know just how deeply we love him and that's why the offense hurt so much. After all, can someone who matters little hurt much? Could it be that, when our attitude toward our offender is one of love, the acknowledgment of our pain is an act of love as well?

Scripture tells us to forgive our offender. We should, however, seek God's timing before approaching the offended/offender with intentions of reconciliation. Be reminded that many years passed before Jacob and Esau were prepared to meet with one another. Indeed, that's not always the case, but we need to be aware that it could be. When the time does comes to lay aside old grudges and move toward your estranged relationship, you'll know it. God will place a peace in your heart about this. There may still be fear in your steps, but you can do this. You can do this because God will give you his strength to do it.

I can do all things through Christ who strengthens me.
Philippians 4:13

Therefore, my dear friends, as you have always obeyed–
not only in my presence, but now much more in my absence–
continue to work out your salvation with fear and trembling,
for it is God who works in you to will and to act according to his good purpose.
Philippians 2:12–13

"Ah, Sovereign Lord,
you have made the heavens and the earth by your great power and outstretched arm.
Nothing is too hard for you."
Jeremiah 32:17

ANY EXCEPTIONS?

Frankly, no. There are no exceptions. And the reason there are no exceptions is because exceptions would put limitations on God's ability to do all things and work his good pleasure through you. You can't limit God. Well, you can, but it will be you doing the limiting, not God. That's a dangerous place to be, choosing your will over God's.

Then Peter came to Jesus and asked,
"Lord how many times shall I forgive my brother when he sins against me?
Up to seven times?"
Jesus answered, "I tell you, not seven times, but seventy-seven times.
Matthew 18:21-22

"Therefore I tell you, whatever you ask for in prayer,
believe that you have received it, and it will be yours.
And when you stand praying, if you hold anything against anyone, forgive him,
so that your Father in heaven may forgive you your sins."
Mark 11:24-26

I need the "so that" part of the verse. I need it because I need God to forgive me my sins. "So that" gives me incentive (lots of incentive) to live a life of forgiveness.

"This, then, is how you should pray:
'Our Father in heaven, hallowed be your name,
your kingdom come, your will be done on earth as it is in heaven.
Give us today our daily bread.
Forgive us our debts, as we also have forgiven our debtors.
And lead us not into temptation, but deliver us from the evil one.'
For if you forgive men when they sin against you,
your heavenly Father will also forgive you.

But if you do not forgive men their sins, your Father will not forgive your sins."
Matthew 6:9–15 (emphasis mine)

What's our responsibility toward a brother or sister in Christ who has wandered from the faith but then turns away from his sin and is now living a lifestyle indicative of repentance? Do we have a tendency to be harder, less forgiving towards the repentant Christian because he or she is a Christian and should have known better? Are we uncomfortable in bringing him or her back into our church, our homes . . . our lives?

The setting of the following story is found in Luke 15:11–16. It goes like this: There was a man with two sons. The younger son asked for his inheritance and the father agreed to give it to him. Next, we see the younger son with money in hand leaving his home of his own free will. But due to immoral and extravagant living, the younger son's money is gone. And isn't it strange that a severe famine occurs just when he's flat broke?

Prodigal

by Ruth Davis

Prodigal, pick yourself up and come home.
Your time in the world was a costly try.
Come back to your Father—you're the apple of his eye.
You left your place—temptation was too great for you.
The bright lights of freedom pulled at your soul.
Somewhere out there you thought happiness awaited you.
If you could only find it in time (in time).
Now you see you left it all behind.
Prodigal, won't you come home?
Prodigal, your Father's arms are open to you.
In your Father's house, the servants have plenty.
While you, his son, have nothing to eat.
If you go home, there's a ring for your finger
And a robe that is rich and brand new (brand new).
Can't you see our Father waits for you?

When he came to his senses, he said,
"How many of my father's hired men have food to spare,
and here I am starving to death!
I will set out and go back to my father and say to him:
Father, I have sinned against heaven and against you.
I am no longer worthy to be called your son;
make me like one of your hired men.
So he got up and went to his father."
Luke 15:17–20a

When he came to his senses. What in the world was this son thinking? How could he have thought so little of a father who had given so much? What (or should I say who) had blinded him to the love that was his? If only he would remember, then surely he would recall how much he was cared for while living with his family. But the desire to live life his way, be separated from his family, and enjoy the pleasures of the world distorted his thinking. It's as though he heard voices telling him, *"Your father is so mad at you. You can't go home. You'll never be forgiven for the mess you've made of your life. And not only that, you've squandered all your wealth. Just stay in the pig-pen. It's where you belong and it's what you deserve."*

Two factors appear to have brought the prodigal "back to his senses":

- the discipline of his choices and
- the love of his father.

Once the son saw where his choices had landed him, he determined to go back to his father and confess his sin.

"But while he was still a long way off,
his father saw him and was filled with <u>compassion</u> for him;
he ran to his son,
threw his arms around him and kissed him."
Luke 15:20

<u>Compassion</u>: Greek, *splagechnizomai* (splangkh-nid'-som-ahee): pity or sympathy, tender mercy, inward affection; strengthened from bowels/spleen

Have you offended someone you know who loves you dearly? We all have. But don't be like Adam and Eve, running away from God trying to cover your sin with some flimsy fig leaves. Run toward your Father. He's good. He's kind. He's waiting to give you a kiss and a hug.

The condemning voices were now silent. In their place was the knowledge that years had been wasted wallowing in a worldly pig-pen. And all the time the wayward son spent living beneath his heritage, his father was at home, waiting to give his child a kiss and a long overdue hug. But there's more, much more.

"But the father said to his servants, 'Quick! Bring the best robe and put it on him. Put a ring on his finger and sandals on his feet. Bring the fattened calf and kill it. Let's have a feast and celebrate. For this son of mine was dead and is alive again; he was lost and is found.' " So they began to celebrate.
Luke 15:22-24

Quick! The best robe, ring and sandals. The best food in the house, cook it. We're having a feast to celebrate the return of my son!

Prodigals, get up and go home! Go home for yourself. Go home for your families. Go home for the blessing that awaits you. Go home for the siblings who might not be so glad to see you; for unless you return, *they* may never hear the words:

" 'My son,' the father said, 'you are always with me,
and everything I have is yours.
But we had to celebrate and be glad,
because this brother of yours was dead and is alive again;
he was lost and is found.' "
Luke 15:31-32

Fellow believers, we must receive back into fellowship the person who has truly repented of his sin. Has the fallen Christian gone to the people whom he's offended and asked their forgiveness? Is he no longer partaking of "pig-pen" behavior? Has he stopped making excuses for his sin? Is he no longer blaming another?

If anyone has caused grief,

he has not so much grieved me (Paul) as he has grieved all of you.
The punishment inflicted on him by the majority is sufficient for him.
Now instead, you ought to forgive and comfort him
so that he will not be overwhelmed by excessive sorrow.
I urge you, therefore, to reaffirm your love for him . . .
in order that Satan mighty not outwit us.
2 Corinthians 2:5–8, 11a

MURDER WITH MALICE

If we've come to believe that Esau wasn't an entirely bad person, then perhaps we can agree about a person who wasn't altogether good, either. To do this let's study the life of a man who was very famous and very loved. We all know him as King David, a man after God's own heart.

Unlike Esau, who was described as a hairy man who "smelled of the field," David's credentials were quite different. I Samuel, Chapter 16 describes David as:

- a handsome man with healthy skin and beautiful to look upon,
- a man gifted in his ability to play the harp,
- a man recognized as a valiant and brave warrior,
- a man gifted with the ability to speak well,
- a man in whom the Spirit of the Lord resides.

Need I say more? David had it all, or at least he had a lot of it! Considered the cream of the crop, David can be likened to the leader of the church youth group, captain of the football team, the young man who wins first place at music and speech competitions. But David, the best of the best and with all his attributes, was not perfect.

In the spring, at the time when kings go off to war,
David sent Joab out with the king's men and the whole Israelite army.
They destroyed the Ammonites and besieged Rabbah.
But David remained in Jerusalem.
One evening David got up from his bed
and walked around on the roof of the palace.
From there he saw a woman bathing. The woman was very beautiful,

and David sent someone to find out about her. The man said, "Isn't this Bathsheba . . . the wife of Uriah the Hittite?"
Then David sent a messenger to get her.
She came to him, and he slept with her. . . Then she went back home.
The woman conceived and sent word to David, saying, "I am pregnant."
2 Samuel 11:1–5 (emphases mine)

David's in quite a dilemma. He's impregnated the wife of another man. Watch now as this desperate king does a despicable thing.

In the morning David wrote a letter to Joab and sent it with Uriah.
In it he wrote, "Put Uriah in the front line where the fighting is fiercest.
Then withdraw from him so he will be struck down and die."
2 Samuel 11:14–15

Prior to David's infidelity with Bathsheba, the stellar reputation of this king was above reproach. Why, a song was even written in honor of his bravery.

"Saul has slain his thousands, and David his tens of thousands."
1 Samuel 18:7

David had slain tens of thousands of men. Yet David was not considered a murderer until he maliciously planned the death of just one man–Uriah, the husband of Bathsheba–thus breaking the sixth commandment of God:

You shall not kill.
Exodus 20:13 (NKJV)

Kill: Hebrew, *ratsach* (raw-tsakh'): to murder a human being
Murder: the unlawful killing of a human life with malice aforethought
Malice aforethought is a predetermination to commit an unlawful act, without just cause or provocation. A murderer intentionally plans the death of a person in order to accomplish personal gain.

You can read the rest of the story of David and Bathsheba in 2 Samuel, Chapters 11 and 12. The bottom line is this:

But the thing David had done displeased the Lord.
2 Samuel 11:27

What led this gifted, brave man of God to murder Uriah? Consider that, after sleeping with Uriah's wife and getting her pregnant, David's new bed partners were guilt and fear. But the real giant, the biggest factor affecting David's decision to murder Uriah was David's unconfessed of adultery sin and an unrepentant heart. Having yet to reestablish fellowship with God, David was left to handle this devilish situation according to his own devices, and murdering Uriah, he thought, was his only way out.

Here's where our heart goes out to David. He's in a predicament like none he's ever experienced. David was a good man with a good heart. He was a dedicated shepherd and obedient son. He grew to become a valiant warrior of the Lord. He had stood tall against tens of thousands of enemies. Before becoming king of Israel, with a rock and a slingshot he killed Goliath. No one was more surprised than David when he found himself *defeated by his own flesh* . . . fallen and drowning in the cesspool of adultery and murder.

Good men fall hard. The disappointment in ourselves is sometimes more than we can bear. Such was the case of David. David had to learn that even kings can fall and find themselves in need of God's mercy.

Then the Lord sent Nathan to speak to David.
"Why have you despised the commandment of the Lord,
to do evil in His sight?
You have killed Uriah the Hittite with the sword;
you have taken his wife to be your wife,
and have killed him with the sword of the people of Ammon.
'Now therefore, the sword shall never depart from your house,
because you have despised Me,
and have taken the wife of Uriah the Hittite to be your wife.'
"Thus says the Lord: Behold, I will raise up adversity against you from
your own house; and I will take your wives before your eyes
and give them to your neighbor,
and he shall lie with your wives in the sight of this sun.
'For you did it secretly, but I will do this thing before all the sun.' "
2 Samuel 12:1–12 (NKJV)

So David said to Nathan,
"I have sinned against the Lord."
2 Samuel 12:13 (NKJV)

David didn't dance around his sin. He said it plain to be heard. "I have sinned against the Lord." Refreshing, isn't it, when a confession is forthright?

And Nathan said to David,
"The Lord also has put away your sin; you shall not die.
However, because by this deed you have given great occasion
to the enemies of the Lord to blaspheme . . .
2 Samuel 12:13b–14a (NKJV)

Yes, David repented of his sin and God put away his sin, but God didn't take away the consequences of adultery with Bathsheba and the murder of Uriah. David's choices had opened the door and given great occasion for the enemies of the Lord to have access to David's family. Though David was forgiven, his "seed of sin" had been sown. This seed would germinate and eventually result in the death of David's first-born child. Such a bitter harvest for David and Bathsheba that year.

What forgiveness lessons have we learned from the lives of Esau, the prodigal son, and David? Esau reveals how beautiful it is when brothers lay aside old grudges, are thankful for God's blessings in their lives, and choose to love one another. The prodigal son enlightens us to the fact that God's wayward children sometimes have trouble remembering the tenderness and affection that awaits them back home. And David's life is a reminder that no man is so great he cannot fall and find himself in need God's mercy. The messages of their lives are, in actuality, very similar. They illustrate the importance of "sowing forgiveness," not only towards those who have offended us but *toward ourselves*. Perhaps God's sixth commandment, "Do not murder," finds its greatest application and is best implemented when we forgive ourselves for the times we've failed God. For if we receive God's gift of forgiveness toward us, shouldn't that make us all the more eager to share it with others?

DELIGHT

Dear friends, since God so loved us, we also ought to love one another.
No one has ever seen God; but if we love one another,
God lives in us and his love is made complete in us.
1 John 4:11-12

Do Not Murder

PRINCIPLES

1. Remembering how much God has forgiven us will help us forgive others.
2. Remembering God's blessings in our lives promotes forgiveness toward others.
3. Emotions of fear or distress while in the presence of a particular person may indicate an offense has occurred.
4. People can change.
5. Wounds can be healed.
6. We can choose to look for the good in people who have hurt us.
7. The ability to forgive is a gift from God that can change our lives.
8. God's love enables us to forsake our own good for the benefit of others.
9. God heals injustices done to us most effectively when we get out of his way.
10. God is compassionate and eager to forgive.
11. It's a God-thing when brothers lay aside old grudges, are thankful for God's blessings, and make the choice to love one another.
12. Wayward children are prone to forget God's good and forgiving nature.
13. No man is so gifted and anointed by God that he cannot fall into sin.
14. We "murder ourselves" when we refuse to forgive ourselves for the times we've failed God.
15. God demonstrated his love for us before we were aware of our sin.

Do Not Murder

DISCUSSION QUESTIONS

1. Verbalize blessings in your life which supersede life's offenses. "Name your plenty."
2. How can remembering God's forgiveness toward us become a basis for forgiving someone who has hurt us?
3. Is there a particular offense you're having a hard time letting go of? Filling in the blank of the following statement might help with that.
   "It cost God as much to forgive me of my offenses as it did to forgive ________________ of his."
4. How you would define true repentance to a friend?
5. As you were reading this chapter, was there a person whose name kept coming to mind?
6. Using the name you identified, focus your mind to look for the good in that person: any true, noble, just, pure, lovely good report, virtuous or praiseworthy attributes you could credit to him? Try hard. You can find it!
7. How is your response to a believer living in sin and an unbeliever living in sin to be_different?
8. Why is it a challenge to give our vengeance to God?
9. What did Esau really want from Jacob?
10. Why does God want you to forgive others up to seventy times seven?
11. Who do you identify with most: Esau, Jacob, the prodigal son, the prodigal's older brother, the prodigal's waiting father, or David?
12. What have you learned about yourself through identifying with this person?

"For I know the plans I have for you," declares the Lord,
"plans to prosper you and not to harm you,
plans to give you hope and a future."

Jeremiah 29:11

Chapter 7
Do Not Commit Adultery
Exodus 20:14

"God Has a Better Plan."

In this chapter you will learn . . .

- of the deaths produced by adultery;
- how a wicked man and a wise man receive correction;
- the characteristics of an adulterous woman and a godly woman;
- the characteristics of a man who lacks judgment and a faithful man.

Hebrew/Greek word studies: death, adultery, fornication, understanding, flee, meek/lowly, betroth

This chapter compares both the virtuous woman and the adulterous woman, along with the man of understanding and the man who lacks judgment. The importance of confessing the sin of adultery and receiving God's gift of mercy is emphasized as well. This chapter encourages the adulterer to lay hold of God's promise of healing, hope, and a future.

King David is an example of a forgiven adulterer. David's life demonstrates that when we accept responsibility for the sin of adultery, God is quick to forgive and provide us with a blessed future. David's life also teaches that though we can be forgiven for this sin, the consequences of our sin can last a lifetime.

The Bluebird Family

by Pat Hinton Menser

The bluebird is busy from morning til night,
She in the home and he on the flight.
Together they plan for the birth of their chicks,
Gathering hay, stubble and sticks.

Persistent in labor, they miss not a beat,
Through rain and the wind, cool or the heat.
They take to their home the tools they will need
To bring forth new life and continue their breed.

New mother and father watch over their nest,
Guarding their eggs from varmints and pests,
Who seek to devour them and rob them of life,
Before they are able to win their own fights.

When babies are born 'tis a time to rejoice
As they open their mouths and cry with their voice,
"We're little. We're hungry. We can't fly alone.
We need our parents to build us a home."

Their daddy is listening and valiantly flies
To streams and to rivers to bring home the prize
Of a worm or an insect, a grub or a fly
He works without grumble–not even a sigh.

Then daddy stands guard over family and home,
While mama feeds babies until they have grown
To the place of their leaving–no longer to stay
In nests built of sticks, stubble and hay.

In our family we refer to Dad, Mom, Aaron and John as the "nuke" (short for "nucleus"). It's an affectionate term that reminds us that, though we're separate individuals, we come together to form one family unit. We're a team that works together and shares in the identity of being the Menser family.

When our son, Aaron, married pretty little Ashley, he was excited about bringing his new bride into the "nuke." And while we love our daughter-in-law dearly and were thrilled for her to become a part of our family, the reality is that she and Aaron formed their own "nuke." I remember receiving a phone call from St. Lucia while they were on their honeymoon when Aaron said to me, "Mama, we're small; it's just the two of us, but we're a family. We're the *new* Menser family."

THE "A" WORD

"It was because your hearts were hard that Moses wrote the law," Jesus replied. "But at the beginning of creation God 'made them male and female.' 'For this reason a man will leave his father and mother and be united to his wife, and the two will become one flesh.' So they are no longer two, but one. Therefore what God has joined together, let man not separate."
Mark 10:5-9

The commandment, "You shall not commit adultery," is perhaps the one commandment that, when broken, has the greatest potential for destroying a marriage. Many times the aftermath of adultery is seemingly irreparable. And though with God nothing is impossible, it does seem that one of life's greatest challenges is that of putting a marriage back together after adultery has ripped it apart.

Have you noticed that our society is more and more accepting of sinful behavior, while the righteous lifestyle is increasingly being ridiculed? This point was driven home to me while watching a current talk show. On this particular show the guests were discussing their promiscuous lifestyle (though they certainly didn't use the word "promiscuous") when a brave lady from the audience stood and made the comment that these people were living in adultery. Immediately, the host of the show became very uncomfortable with the word "adultery" and made a quick point of defending the guest's choice of lifestyle.

Mind another illustration? When talking with my father about a mutual acquaintance (who happened to be living with his girlfriend), Daddy tried to refer to our friend's live-in girlfriend in a non-offensive way. With noticeable difficulty, he finally stuttered the words, "You know, so-and-so's, uh, ah, ummm . .. I don't know what to call her."

"Do you mean his adulteress?" I asked.

"Well, yeah, I guess that pretty well says it," he replied.

According to *Random House Dictionary*, *adulterate* means "to debase by adding inferior materials or elements, to make impure by admixture." When you adulterate something you've added an inferior substance into something that was once pure. By doing this you've debased, corrupted or lessened the value of the pure substance. Gold is adulterated when other metals are added to it.

Yes, "adultery" is still a word, but one becoming more and more obsolete, sounding almost antiquated to our modern ears. Why is that? We know God clearly says, "You shall not commit adultery." If God used the word "adultery" in one of his commandments, then surely it's not God who wants this word eradicated from our vocabulary.

The truth sometimes hurts. Sin always hurts God and the people involved. The fact that sin hurts and that talking about sin makes people uncomfortable should come as no surprise.

When tempted, no one should say, "God is tempting me."
For God cannot be tempted by evil, nor does he tempt anyone;
but each one is tempted when, by his own evil desire, he is dragged away and enticed.
Then, after desire has deceived, it gives birth to sin:
and sin, when it is full-grown, gives birth to death.
James 1:13–15

Scripture teaches that, when sin is full-grown, it produces death. Yet many reading this text have committed adultery and are obviously still alive. So what does "gives birth to death" really mean?

. . . and sin, when it is full-grown, brings forth death.
James 1:15b

Death: Greek, *thanatos* (than'-at-os): to die in a literal or *figurative* sense

Has the Lord not made them one? In flesh and spirit they are his.
And why one? Because he was seeking godly offspring.
So guard yourself in your spirit and do not break faith with the wife of your youth.
"I hate divorce," says the Lord God of Israel. . .
(So guard yourself in your spirit, and do not break faith.
Malachi 2:15–16

D-I-V-O-R-C-E

By Pat Menser
(A collective perspective of children of divorce)
(Malachi 2:15–16)
They say that they still love me and that nothing's really changing.
It's just that they can't live as one and their lives need rearranging.
I thought they meant we'd take a trip, or maybe buy a car.
Oh, what a shock when I found out just how things really are.

I learned that Mama has a boyfriend and, well, Daddy's gone again.
The fact is that I'm all alone in a place I've never been.
I have to sew on buttons and the brownies—I must bake.
'Cause Mama thinks I'm big enough to cook and stay up late.

But really, I'm still little, and I wish she'd tuck me in
Instead of fixing up and going out on dates with him.
I used to have a dresser, and the drawers were nice and full.
Socks and shirts were all in place—clean underwear the rule.

But now, my things are scattered—some are here and some are there.
I never know from day to day just what I'll have to wear.
I'm learning not to plan my days—to try, believe or trust.
You're just not as disappointed if you don't expect too much.
I hate divorce.

Death from sexual sin takes many forms. When a marriage dies, children of divorce are often wounded and scarred for the rest of their lives. Adultery oftentimes results in strained physical and mental health. Divorce can take a heavy toll on finances, and now, with the increase of sexually transmitted diseases and death due to AIDS, we're forced to acknowledge that adultery has the potential of bringing death in the literal sense as well. In order to avoid these death traps, we must be clear about what sexual sin is.

You shall not commit adultery.
Exodus 20:14

Adultery: Hebrew, *naaph* (naw-af'): to break wedlock
Adultery: voluntary sexual intercourse of a married person with someone other than his/her lawful spouse (*Random House Dictionary*)

Gold is adulterated when other metals are added to it. That's the essence of adultery: bringing a foreign person into a marriage and contaminating its purity.

A word often used interchangeably with the word "adultery" is the word "fornication."

But fornication, and all uncleanness or covetousness,
Let it not even be named among you, as is fitting for saints; . . .
Ephesians 5:3 (NKJV)

Fornication: Greek, *porneia* (porn-ni'-ah): to indulge in unlawful lust, to act the harlot or whore
Fornication: voluntary sexual intercourse between two unmarried persons, or two persons not married to each other (*Random House Dictionary*)

Fornication is the word used to describe sexual relations outside of marriage. Grace is a word used to describe God's relationship with us.

But where sin increased, grace increased all the more.
Romans 5:20b (emphasis mine)

Let's stay here a while. Got a pen? *Grace*. I looked up some synonyms for this word:

mercy kindness benevolence compassion tenderness gentleness

Maybe you could add a few more.

Grace describes God. Grace encompasses the very nature of our Heavenly Father. Many, however, don't understand how "gracious" the Lord truly is. We tend to see God as full of anger and revenge, and as a result we're fearful of taking our mistakes to him. Perhaps we need to be reminded that God's greatest power is seen in his ability to forgive.

God is eager to pardon our sin, specifically the sin of fornication/adultery. He's simply waiting for us to be honest with him and with ourselves. He knows that true healing cannot take place until our wound is opened and thoroughly cleansed. Confessing our sin is much like pouring peroxide over an infected wound. It may sting at first and be a little messy as the infection and dirt fizz away. Yes, confession will likely be a painful process, but for our ultimate healing God encourages us to pour it on!

"I COMPESS, I COMPESS, I DID IT"

When my sons were young, they often reminded me of two tiger cubs, wrestling and clawing and vying for dominance. Aaron was older and obviously the physically stronger of the two. But Little John, as we affectionately called him, had his arsenal as well.

I remember one day hearing the all too familiar sounds of yet another brawl. I'd had it. I told them both to go to the bathroom and stay there while Mama went to her bedroom to pray and ask the Holy Spirit how to deal with their fighting (should have done a lot more of that, by the way). Boy, was God ever quick to give me insight that day. I went back downstairs and told my little tomcats, "Here's the deal: I don't know which of you started this fight, but if the guilty boy doesn't own up to his behavior, I will give both of you a hard spanking. However, if the person who started this fight will admit it, then your spanking will be an easy one.

Now, Mama is going back to her bedroom and give you some time to think about it."

It's been over twenty years since that day, but I still smile when I remember going back into the bathroom and seeing Little John's dark brown head tucked deep into his chest and his three-year-old little hand rising ever so slowly, "I compess, I compess, I did it."

Are you tired of wrestling with God about the sin of adultery? Are you ready to "compess" that you did it? The rest of the story is that Aaron was sent out of the bathroom while I dealt privately with John's behavior. As soon as the door was shut, my sweet though guilty, beautiful, precious little toddler willingly leaned over the toilet seat, and waited for the wooden spoon. Want to know the blessing that came out of this incident for me? It was that John trusted me. He knew how much I loved him and that I didn't find any pleasure in hurting him. He knew I didn't want to punish him but that I had to because he deserved it. That day, it was a soft spoon that came his way.

If we confess our sins, He is faithful and just to forgive us our sins
and to cleanse us from all unrighteousness.
1 John 1:9 (NKJV)

Cleanse: Greek, *katharizo* (kath-ar-id'-zo): to purge, to purify, to make clean; clear, pure
Free from impure admixture, without blemish, spotless (Vine, 103)

A PROPER INTRODUCTION

Those who have suffered the consequences of adultery would surely testify to the pain it causes. These people, however, weren't looking for pain when they met up with Adultery. Quite the contrary. The master of lies told them that sexual relations outside of marriage would bring happiness and bliss and, indeed, for a moment their lust did bring physical pleasure. But what Adultery didn't tell them is how they would feel after the excitement of their lust had calmed down.

If Adultery had been an honest person, he would have introduced himself something like this: "Hello, my name is Adultery. My mission is to entrap you for life. I will accomplish my goal by bringing pleasure to your flesh that will last only a few short moments. Once you've tasted my perverse and illicit sex, you won't be satisfied with the lawful kind anymore. Sex with your spouse will seem painfully boring. And now that you're enslaved to my sexual substitute, *I'll be the one experiencing pleasure* as I continually remind you of our time together. Oh, but my ecstasy doesn't end there. The ultimate purpose of luring you into my bed is to place such guilt and shame on you that you'll think yourself of no value to God or use for his kingdom."

John 8:44 tells us the truth about this liar:

You belong to your father, the devil, and you want to carry out your father's desire.
He was a murderer from the beginning, not holding to the truth,
for there is no truth in him. When he lies, he speaks his native language,
for he is a liar and the father of lies.

Oh, how appealing the serpent of seduction can be. Her voluptuous venom paralyzes the mind of her victim. Enticed by her scent . . . mesmerized by her charm . . . captivated by her performance . . . her prey becomes disoriented, resulting in a noticeable lack of:

Understanding/Judgment: Hebrew, *leb* (labe): judgment, courage, wisdom

I saw among the simple, I noticed among the young men,
a youth who lacked judgment.
Proverbs 7:7

Have you ever tried to reason with someone who is intoxicated? Do you remember feeling as though your words were neither appreciated nor, for the most part, even heard? A drunkard doesn't want to listen to reason. Why? Because a drunkard wants to be left alone to enjoy his stupor.

Likewise, the person "drunk with lust" often resents being directed toward spiritual sobriety. He enjoys the sensual, seductive voice of lust whispering in his ear, "Stolen water is sweet. Food eaten in secret is the best kind."

Notice the difference between how a mocker and a wise man react to being corrected:

Do not rebuke a mocker or he will hate you;
rebuke a wise man and he will love you.
Proverbs 9:8

Perhaps, either personally or as the result of another's actions, you've endured the pain and subsequent death that adultery brings. Because you know the devastation of adultery, you may want to show a loved one involved in adultery the error of his or her way. Be forewarned that your genuine concern may be misconstrued: for until the "mocker" becomes a "wise man," he may insult, abuse, even hate you for noticing the instability in his life due to his relationship with Adultery.

THE FORGIVEN ADULTERER

King David is an example of how adultery can capture even the best of men. As you'll recall, God used the prophet, Nathan, to help David see his sin. And it's here where the words "Rebuke a wise man and he will love you. Instruct a wise man and he will be wiser still" (Proverbs 9:9) come to life. David's response to being corrected by his spiritual mentor gives us a glimpse into the heart of a great king.

Then David said to Nathan,
"I have sinned against the Lord."
2 Samuel 12:13a

A lesson from the life of David is: *there's life after adultery*. It seems, however, that the quality of life is contingent upon the heart-felt attitude of the adulterer. Could it be that David's willingness to clearly confess his adultery is what enabled him to recover from its consequences? Does confession hasten healing? These questions are asked to encourage you to examine your past and the way in which you might have dealt with sexual sin.

If you've committed adultery, have you taken full responsibility for your actions? As firmly and forthrightly as I can type these words, let me emphatically say, "Don't skirt around a complete confession of sexual sin." Justifying, condoning, or half-way admissions of guilt will not clear the way for your healing or for your testimony to be useful for God's kingdom. As long as you are in any way protecting your former lover or any "vows" you may have made to one another, you are, in essence, still in a relationship with that person. Break it off, completely. Confess your sin, totally. This is the only way the infection of sexual sin can be cleansed from your life.

Please note that David didn't search for a detour from the road to true repentance. David made the deliberate choice to face his sin–head on–and then give that sin to God. David called his adultery a sin against God (2 Samuel 12:13a). Perhaps there are those who need to follow his example.

A second lesson David's life teaches is to *accept the consequences of our sin.* In the case of David, adultery resulted in the literal death of his first-born son. Of course David wanted the outcome to be different. Scripture tells that David pleaded with the Lord on behalf of his son. He spent his nights lying on the ground, refusing to eat any food. But once the verdict was in, David accepted it. David didn't live in the past, trying to resurrect what his sin had killed. He chose to move forward with his life. Soon he and Bathsheba would be parents to another baby boy whom they would name Solomon.

A third lesson we can learn from the way David handled his sin of adultery is that *forgiveness provides hope for a blessed future.* Yes, adultery demanded the life of David's son, but God's forgiveness gave David hope that one day he would reunited with the very son whom his sin had killed.

He (David) answered, "While the child was still alive, I fasted and wept.
I thought, 'Who knows? The Lord may be gracious to me and let the child live.'
But now that he is dead, why should I go on fasting? Can I bring him back again?
I will go to him, but he will not return to me."
2 Samuel 12:22–23

Now, we're about to ask Scripture to describe what an adulterous woman looks like. And if, once we've identified her, we're tempted to point a finger, let's first be careful that it's one of compassion.

A Lavender Lady

by Pat Menser
(*2 Corinthians 1:3–4*)

My vase was made in China; she is delicate and rare.
Yellow, rose, and lavender have colored her with care.
Her patterns are most intricate, with florals, ferns and vines.
An ancient art is captured if you'll read between her lines.

One day while I was dusting, My vase fell from her shelf.
She broke in many pieces and it saddens Me to tell
You of the pain that I was feeling—the grief that gripped My heart,
As My vase who had much value was now shattered—torn apart.

I quickly searched for all her pieces—the ones ripped from My vase.
Then, carefully, I carried them back to a safer place
Where I began the healing process of restoring to My treasure,
Her self-esteem and dignity—her place of worth and measure.

I gladly matched her scattered pieces, then I glued each one in place.
I held her near—I wiped her tears—until there was no trace
That My vase was ever injured—that she once was torn apart.
"Twas only I who saw her with her open . . . broken . . . heart."

And because My vase has suffered and has felt the pain of life
I handle her more tenderly than otherwise I might.
For I understand her weakness, and I know her sorrow song,
A wounded past . . . a brokenness . . . a fragile vase made strong.

Now we're ready to uncover the characteristics of an adulterous woman.

For the lips of an adulteress drip honey, and her speech is smoother than oil;
She gives no thought to the way of life; her paths are crooked, but she knows it not.
She is loud and defiant, her feet never stay at home;
I have perfumed my bed with myrrh, aloes and cinnamon.
Come, let's drink deep of love till morning; let's enjoy ourselves with love!
With persuasive words she led him astray; she seduced him with her smooth talk.

"This is the way of an adulteress:
She eats and wipes her mouth and says, 'I've done nothing wrong.' "
Proverbs 5:3, 6; 7:11a, 17–18, 21; 30:20

Scripture pulls the covers of adultery all the way down for us, further revealing her hidden, bitter stench:

But in the end she is bitter as gall, sharp as a double-edged sword.
Her feet go down to death; her steps lead straight to the grave.
You will say, "How I hated discipline! How my heart spurned correction!
I would not obey my teachers or listen to my instructors.
I have come to the brink of utter ruin in the midst of the whole assembly."
Do not lust in your heart after her beauty or let her captivate you with her eyes,
for the prostitute reduces you to a loaf of bread,
and the adulteress preys upon your very life.
Proverbs 5:4–5, 12–14; 6:26

AVOIDING ADULTERY

As tempting as the adulterous woman can be, there is a way to escape her charm. This point is illustrated in the life of Joseph, son of Jacob.

Genesis, Chapter 37 tells how the sons of Jacob became so jealous of Jacob's love for Joseph that they conspired to sell Joseph into Egyptian slavery. After years of slavery, Joseph was promoted to chief attendant in the house of his Egyptian master, Potiphar. And it was here where Potiphar's wife displayed her adulterous character.

Now Joseph was well-built and handsome,
and after a while his master's wife took notice of Joseph and said,
"Come to bed with me!"
Genesis 39:6b-7

This woman was pleading with Joseph. She was hungry for sexual pleasure. One can imagine her lips, dripping with honey, her speech, smoother than oil, her dress, surely provocative, her desire for intimacy, shameless, and the aroma coming from her perfumed bed–oh, so appealing. And this was not a one-time offer. Oh, no. Adultery pursued Jacob day after day after day. . .

And though she spoke to Joseph day after day,
he refused to go to bed with her or even be with her.
Genesis 39:10

Joseph escaped the claws of this harlot by doing the only thing that could free him:

But he left his cloak in her hand and ran out of the house.
Flee from sexual immorality.
All other sins a man commits are outside his body,
But whoever sins sexually, sins against his own body.
Genesis 29:12b, 1 Corinthians 6:18

Flee: Greek, *pheugo* (fyoo′-go): to run away, vanish or escape

Samson

By Pat Menser
(Inspired by *Judges, Chapter 16,* and Robert Frost's poem, *"The Road Less Traveled"*)

'Twas agony that pierced my heart the hour I realized
My son was headed down a path that led to his demise.
I cried, "My son, oh can't you see this road that leads to less,
Is full of sorrow, tears and pain, but most of all—regret?"

Regret for where you could have gone, for how it might have been,
If only you would hear God's voice and not the praise of men,
'Twas pride that held you captive—the acclaim of men's applause,
They lied to you then used you for a worldly, lesser cause.

For men care not of God's great plan that leads away from sin.
They only want to take from you the strength that lies within,
Your honor and your stature, your training and pure heart,
They wish to have it for themselves, leaving you with just a part

Of how it was before you wandered—where you were before you veered
From the path of God's own choosing—Oh, my son, my son, please hear!
Shake the shackles of your slumber; drop the bands from off your feet,
Give the world the road well-traveled, and let God lead you to peace.
It will make all the difference.

At the window of my house I looked out through the lattice.
I saw among the simple, I noticed among the young men,
a youth who lacked judgment.
He was going down the street near her corner,
walking along in the direction of her house at twilight,
as the day was fading, as the dark of night set in.
Proverbs 7:6-9 (emphases mine)

Notice how sexual sin baits her victim and then slowly reels him in: Down the street>>>Near her corner>>>In the direction of her house . . .

Then out came a woman to meet him,
dressed like a prostitute and with crafty intent.
All at once he followed her like an ox going to the slaughter,
like a deer stepping into a noose till an arrow pierces his liver,
like a bird darting into a snare, little knowing it will cost him his life.
Proverbs 7:10, 22–23

The first mistake men who lack judgment make is going near the source of sexual sin. They "walk along in the direction of her house" as the day is fading and as the dark of night sets in. Not Joseph. He ran in the *opposite* direction.

Being the mother of two now grown sons, I've lived the last twenty-plus years placed squarely in the world of testosterone. I know testosterone. And I fondly recall the multitudes of weightlifting, football-playing, hungry, sweaty, maturing male teenagers who've watched TV in our basement, sacked out on our couch, and cleaned out our refrigerator.

I loved every one of them. I loved feeding their faces and listening to their girlfriend woes. One young man in particular felt free to talk to me about sexual matters. Without going into a lot of detail, I felt comfortable sharing with him the best method of birth-control he could possess, and I used the Joseph story (Genesis 39:12) as the basis for my advice. "Run!" I'd say. "Keep a good pair of running shoes with you at all times and be ready to run." Years later this special young man said these words to me: "Mrs. Menser, I've still got my shoes on. It's been tough. I've come close to taking them off. But so far my running shoes are working."

THE VIRTUOUS WOMAN

And the Lord God said, "It is not good that man should be alone;
I will make him a helper comparable to him."
Genesis 2:18 (NKJV)

Helper/Helpmeet: Hebrew, *azar* (ay′-zer): to surround, to protect or aid

God created Eve as a helper who would surround Adam with her love, and aid him with her strength and protection. The same word, "helper," is used to describe God in Psalm 20:2, 33:20, 115:9, 121:1–2, and 2 Chronicles 25:8. Just as God is our Helper, surrounding us with his strength, love and protection, so are women created to be a "helper" to their husbands.

I also want women to dress modestly, with decency and propriety,
not with braided hair or gold or pearls or expensive clothes, but with good deeds,
appropriate for women who profess to worship God.
Your beauty should not come from outward adornment,
such as braided hair and the wearing of gold jewelry or fine clothes.
Instead, it should be that of your inner self,
the unfading beauty of a gentle and quiet spirit,
which is of great worth in God's sight.
For this is the way the holy women of the past who put their hope in God
used to make themselves beautiful.
1 Timothy 2:9–10, 1 Peter 3:3–5a

Modest: Greek, *kosmios* (kos′-mee-os): orderly, of good behavior
Some of the synonyms I found for *modest* include: humble, unassuming, reserved, decent, chaste, clean, spotless, pure, immaculate, simple, unadorned, discreet, and plain.

Please girls, please listen to truth: God doesn't determine our beauty by the hairstyle we choose or the type of jewelry or clothes we wear. We don't need to lengthen our necklines or shorten our hems to be beautiful. God defines beauty in terms of a gentle and quiet spirit, which he says is of great worth to him. God likes women who dress modestly and put their hope in him, as did the holy women of the past.

Charm is deceptive, and beauty is fleeting;
but a woman who fears the Lord is to be praised.
Proverbs 31:30

THE HUMBLE MAN

The same people who say feminine beauty is determined by the shape of our legs and the size of our busts are telling men their beauty is all about macho and muscles. But God doesn't use these criteria. His opinion of masculine beauty isn't based on a man's physical features but rather upon the attributes of a specific Person.

Take my yoke upon you, and learn of me;
for I am meek and lowly in heart and ye shall find rest unto your souls.
Matthew 11:29 (KJV)

> Meek: Greek, *praos* (prah'-os): mild, humble, meek, gentle
> Meekness "consists not in a person's outward behavior only; nor yet in his relations to his fellow-men; as little as in his mere natural disposition. Rather it is an inwrought *grace of the soul*; and the exercises of it are first and chiefly towards God. It is the temper of spirit in which we accept his dealings with us as good, and therefore without disputing or resisting" (Vine, 401; italics mine).

Is there anyone more beautiful to you than your own child? Can there be anyone more beautiful to God than his son? When looking at Jesus we see masculine beauty as that of a gentle and humble heart. Is there a young man living in your house? If so, I urge you to look beyond his broadening shoulders and deepening voice–into the spirit living within. Just as his body is maturing physically, his spirit wants to mature as well. And just as his body needs nourishment, his spirit needs training in the discipline of meekness in order to grow into the likeness of Christ. And let's be sure to notice that the benefit of a meek heart is a soul at rest.

LUST WON'T WAIT!

King David was noticeably lacking in judgment when he committed adultery with Bathsheba. Sad to say, David's son, Amnon, followed in his father's sexual footsteps.

2 Samuel, Chapter 13 (paraphrased):

"Amnon, son of David, why does your skin hang from your bones?" asked Jonadab. "It's not fitting that the King's son should be in such distress. Is there a disease upon you?"

"I am vexed with love," replied Amnon.

"Who has done this to you? Surely you can have any woman in the kingdom."

"It is Tamar, the sister of Absolom," answered Amnon. "Her virginity torments me. I have tried to have my way with her, but to no avail. I think of nothing but the beauty of Tamar."

"Be grieved no longer," Jonadab replied. "Fair Tamar will lie with you tonight!"

Jonadab devised a plan that would play upon the sympathies of Amnon's father, King David. In accordance with Jonadab's plan, Amnon requested that his father, King David, ask Tamar to come to the house to prepare a meal for him. And so, at the request of her father (for Amnon and Tamar were half-brother and -sister), Tamar went to Amnon's house and kneaded him some bread.

Amnon took more than bread from Tamar. He took her virginity. With this prized possession under his belt, you'd think Amnon would be content.

Then Amnon hated her with intense hatred.
In fact, he hated her more than he had loved her.
Amnon said to her, "Get up and get out!"
2 Samuel 13:15

But Amnon, we don't understand. Prior to being intimate with Tamar, you told Jonadab you were "sick with love." Now that you've had your way with her, you say you "hate her more than you had loved her."

The life of Amnon teaches us that lust is a very powerful and controlling force. In the case of Amnon, his lust for Tamar outweighed his natural need for food and the desire to take care of his physical health. Consumed with lust, he lost his appetite for food and became physically sick, resulting in a lean, haggard appearance.

Indeed, lust wants to destroy the perpetrator, but lust has no conscience in destroying its victim as well. Consider poor Tamar, the unwilling victim of Amnon's lust. Scripture tells us that, following Tamar's rape, she put ashes on her head, tore her robe, put her hands on her head and went away weeping loudly (2 Samuel 13:19).

Amnon followed a path of sin cleared and given entry into his life by his own father, King David. When did this trailblazing take place? Before Amnon was even born . . . on an evening when King David got up from his bed, walked around the roof of his palace, and gazed upon the wife of another man (2 Samuel 11:2). A lesson to be learned from Amnon is that the sins of a parent all too often continue into the next generation.

TRUE LOVE WAITS

You'll recall that Jacob lied to his father, Isaac, and defrauded his brother, Esau. But in the area of "waiting for true love," Jacob's virtue shines brightly.

Jacob was in love with Rachel and said,
"I'll work for you seven years in return for your younger daughter Rachel."
Laban said, "It's better that I give her to you than to some other man.
Stay here with me."
So Jacob served seven years to get Rachel,
but they seemed like only a few days to him because of his love for her.
Genesis 29:18–20

Male or female, if you have even a hint of romance running through your veins, you have to love the words: *but they seemed like only a few days to him because of his love for her* (Genesis 29:20). Can you feel Jacob's love for Rachel these many centuries later? That's true love. It waits. It lasts. It endures.

Listen now as God conveys his commitment to you:

I will betroth you to me forever;
I will betroth you in righteousness and justice, in love and compassion.
I will betroth you in faithfulness, and you will acknowledge the Lord.
Hosea 2:19-20

> Betroth: Hebrew, *'aras* (aw-ras'): engage for matrimony
> "Betrothal is an ancient custom dating from biblical times when marriages were arranged by a parent or guardian. It was considered the beginning of marriage, and since it was legally binding, the pledge could not be broken except by a bill of divorce. This is the reason why Joseph is referred to as the husband of Mary in Matthew 1:19." (Freeman, 397).

Do you remember the anticipation you felt as you waited for your wedding day? Was your desire for intimacy almost unbearable? Given that we're created in the image of God, do you think it's possible God has the same feelings toward you?

Perhaps in the past the lust of your flesh wed you to someone other than God. This relationship may have left you feeling empty and not at all satisfied. Maybe now you're feeling drawn to a deeper love, a purer form of commitment, a holy and sacred relationship. Dear friend, this is God's love—courting you, wooing you to be betrothed to him. Please don't miss the opportunity to be united to the One who loves you the most and has waited patiently for you to accept his proposal.

You are invited to attend the wedding of
(your name) _________________________and the Lord Jesus Christ.

Here's how to RSVP to the above invitation:

You must understand that God wants you to have eternal life, living forever in heaven with him.

For God so loved the world that he gave his one and only son,
that whoever believes in him shall not perish but have eternal life.
John 3:16

Everyone falls short of the holiness of God. No one is without sin. But you are justified (rendered innocent) of your sinful nature through the sacrifice of the sinless life of Christ. Forgiving you of your sins is God's free gift to you. It's called grace because you can't earn it.

For all have sinned and fall short of the glory of God,
and are justified freely by his grace
through the redemption that came by Christ Jesus.
Romans 3:23–24

God didn't wait for you to get your life in order or to become good enough before he would give you his love. God loved you while you were still living in sin. God's Word says he knew you and loved you before you were even born.

But God demonstrates his own love for us in this:
While we were still sinners, Christ died for us.
Romans 5:8

You won't go to heaven because you believe there is a God. The devil's demons believe there is a God, but that doesn't mean they've committed their lives to God (James 2:19). In order for salvation to take place, you must believe in your heart that God raised Jesus from the dead. You then commit your life to Jesus, exchanging your sinful nature for his sinless nature, entrusting your eternal well-being to him.

DELIGHT

That if you confess with your mouth, "Jesus is Lord,"
and believe in your hear that God raised him from the dead,
you will be saved.
Romans 10:9

God is asking you to act now and say "yes" to his offer of salvation.

I tell you, now is the time of God's favor, now is the day of salvation.
2 Corinthians 6:2b[1]

[1] Emphases are mine.

Do Not Commit Adultery

PRINCIPLES

1. A wise person runs away from sexual activity outside of marriage.
2. A person who lacks judgment runs toward sexual activity outside of marriage.
3. Sin leads to death.
4. Confession cleanses.
5. Adultery changes a marriage.
6. Adultery changes the lives of children of divorce.
7. The pleasure of sexual sin is fleeting.
8. The consequences of sexual sin are life-long.
9. Satan's native language is lying. There is no truth in him.
10. God's plan for your life is to give you hope and a future.
11. There is no sin larger than God's grace.
12. There is life after adultery.
13. God's patience is meant to lead you to repentance.
14. God would have you act now, saying "yes" to his offer of marriage.

Do Not Commit Adultery

DISCUSSION QUESTIONS

1. James 1:13-15 helps answer the following questions.
   When you're being tempted to sin, who or what is tempting you? (v. 14)
   What happens when you give in to your evil desires? (v. 15)
   What is the end result of sin? (v. 15)

2. Jeremiah 29:11 tells you:
   The thoughts and plans God has toward you.
   What God wants to give you.

3. Proverbs 9:7–9 contrasts the way a wicked man and a wise man receives correction.

4. What do you think gave Joseph the strength to resist the advances of Potiphar's wife?

5. What are some excuses King David could have given Nathan to avoid taking responsibility for his sin with Bathsheba?

6. 2 Samuel 12:22–24. In your own words, describe how David responded to the consequences of his adultery with Bathsheba and murder of Uriah.

7. 2 Samuel 12:23. How do you think David's desire "to go to him (his son)" affected the rest of David's life?

8. Let's not forget that Uriah's family was also the victim of David's sin. What effect do you think David's sin had upon Uriah's family?

9. Romans 5:20b. Paraphrase your thoughts about grace increasing over sin.

10. Can you identify a specific time when you said "yes" to Jesus?

But if we have food and clothing, we will be content with that.

1 Timothy 6:8

Chapter 8

Do Not Steal

Exodus 20:15

"You're Rich Already."

In this chapter you will learn:

- the role faith in Abraham's ability to trust God to provide for his needs;
- a summary of the life of Lot;
- why the love of money can be a substitute for contentment in our relationship with God;
- the responsibility parents have to train their children in the ways of the Lord.

Hebrew/Greek word studies: steal, command, keep, inheritance, faith

This chapter teaches how the love of money is often a substitute for finding security in our relationship with God. An intimate relationship with God produces a sense of contentment and satisfaction in our lives. Thus, our inclination to love money or to want to rob from others is lessened when we experience our true "spiritual wealth."

Abraham knew God and was confident God would bless him wherever he was called to live. Scripture tells us that Abraham was a rich man (Genesis 13:1–2). But before Abraham could claim his inheritance, he had to have faith in God and go where God led him.

By faith Abraham,
when called to go to a place he would later receive as his inheritance,
obeyed and went, even though he did not know where he was going.
But my righteous one will live by faith.
Hebrews 11:8–9, 10:38a

In this chapter we'll consider that oftentimes a person steals when he doesn't differentiate between the desires of his flesh and the desires of his spirit. We'll also gain insight into how easy it is to satisfy our flesh when it's our spirit that is starving.

"Melkik . . . Melchisik . . . Oh, Father, what *was* his name?" asked Isaac.

"It was Melchizedek, the King of Salem," replied Abraham.

"Please, Father, tell me the story. It is my favorite, yet it is the one I understand least," said Isaac.

Tenderly Abraham replied, "My son, even I do not fully understand its meaning, for it is difficult to know when the story of Melchizedek actually began. It is said his tent is pitched in Salem, which is a reference to the city of Jerusalem. He's been called the 'King of Salem,' the 'King of Peace,' and the 'Prince of Peace.' "

"Father, why did he show himself to *you*?" asked Isaac.

"I believe he appeared at the command of Jehovah," answered Abraham. "Let me explain. Many times I have told you how the Lord blessed my nephew, Lot, and me with an abundance of livestock, silver and gold. Our wealth grew until the land could no longer support its weight. At that time I learned my herdsmen were quarreling with the herdsmen of Lot. So I said to Lot:

'Let's not have any quarreling between you and me,
or between your herdsmen and mine, for we are brothers.
Is not the whole land before you? Let's part company.
If you go to the left, I'll go the right; if you go to the right, I'll go to the left.'
Lot looked up and saw that the whole plain of Jordan was well watered,
like the garden of the Lord, like the land of Egypt, toward Zoar.
(This was before the Lord destroyed Sodom and Gomorrah.)
Genesis 13:8–10

"And so it was that Lot chose the whole plain of Jordan," said Abraham.

"Please hurry, Father, and get to the good part," said Isaac.

Abraham smiled and replied, "You are right, my son. The word of the Lord is good. You'll remember that after Lot and I had parted ways, the Lord spoke to me again and said:

'Lift up your eyes from where you are and look north and south, east and west.

All the land that you see I will give to you and your offspring forever.
I will make your offspring like the dust of the earth,
so that if anyone could count the dust, then your offspring could be counted.'
Genesis 13:14b–16

"Dear Isaac, it saddens me to say Lot pitched his tents near the city of Sodom. Now it was well known the men of Sodom had wicked hearts and did not serve the God Most High (Genesis 13:13). As you might expect, war came to Sodom while Lot and his family were living there," continued Abraham.

"Father, you were so brave," said Isaac.

"Oh, son, it's not my courage you're to revere. It was the strength of Jehovah," replied Abram. "When I heard Lot was taken captive, I called 318 of my trained men and we, along with the king of Sodom, the king of Gomorrah, the king of Admah, the king of Zeboiim and the king of Bela, pursued the enemy as far as Dan. Because the Lord was with us, we recovered all that was stolen. We then brought Lot and his possessions, the women and all the other people back to their homes in Sodom," said Abraham (Genesis 14:14-16).

"But when did you see Melchiside . . . Melkisid . . . " asked Isaac.

"You mean M-E-L-C-H-I-Z-E-D-E-K," Abraham offered.

"Yes, Father, when did you see *him*?" asked Isaac.

"It was when the king of Sodom and I were returning from our victory in the Valley of Shaveh. We looked, and over the horizon we saw Melchizedek bringing out bread and wine. As he approached, he spoke these words:

'Blessed be Abram by God Most High, Creator of heaven and earth.
And blessed be God Most High, who delivered your enemies into your hand.'
Genesis 14:19b–20a

"I then gave Melchizedek a tenth of everything," said Abraham.

"I know this part!" shouted Isaac. "Next you were tempted by the king of Sodom when he said, 'Give me the people and *keep the goods for yourself*.'" (Genesis 14:21).

"You've listened well," said Abraham. "But do you know the rest of the story?"

"I forgot," said Isaac.

"Take heed to these words, my son, and learn of their wisdom, for they will guide you long after my bones have been laid to rest," instructed

Abraham. "When the king of Sodom tempted me to take that which was not mine, I said to him:

"I have raised my hand to the Lord, God Most High, Creator of heaven and earth,
and have taken an oath that I will accept nothing belonging to you,
not even a thread or the thong of a sandal, so that you will never be able to say,
'I made Abram rich.'"
Genesis 14:22-23

"After this," said Abraham, "the word of the Lord came to me in a vision and said:

"Do not be afraid, Abram. I am your shield, your very great reward.
A son coming from your own body will be your heir."
Genesis 15:1, 4b

"Dear Isaac, you are that son, an heirloom given to me from God—a very great reward," said Abraham.

Nestling in his father's arms, Isaac replied, "Father, I love the story of Melchizedek."

"Not as much as I, my son. Not nearly as much."

It must be noted that Abraham's life of obedience didn't end or, for that matter, even begin in the Valley of Shaveh when he encountered Melchizedek. To understand this truth, let's turn the pages of our Bible back to Genesis, Chapters 11 and 12, where we'll find Abraham's journey of obedience beginning in the land of Haran, when he heard the voice of the Lord say:

"Leave your country, your people and your father's household
and go to the land I will show you."
Genesis 12:1

And without faith it is impossible to please God,
because anyone who comes to him must believe that he exists
and that he rewards those who earnestly seek him.
Hebrews 11:6

Faith: Greek, *pistis* (pis'-tis): to have confidence in, to trust and yield to, to be convinced; reliance upon God for salvation, persuasion, constancy in such a profession

It is vital that we be clear about something: having faith in God is much more than believing God exists.

You believe that there is one God. You do well.
Even the demons believe–and tremble!
James 2:19 (NKJV)

More than just believing there is one God, faith *in God* means we've exchanged our lives for his. We have confidence in him and are convinced we can rely on him for our salvation. Like Abraham, our faith in God motivates us to obey and go. The reason we can do this is because we've given our hearts to God, and he softens them in a way that causes us to actually *delight in obeying him* (more on this topic in Chapter 11).

I love those who love me,
and those who seek me find me.
Proverbs 8:17 (emphasis mine)

Seeking to find God, delighting in him, tasting his word and enjoying its flavor–our eyes are opened to see that the Lord is good! (Psalm 34:8). This is what it means to be rich: this is the truest form of wealth, for Abraham, for us, and for those who will follow after us.

The ordinances of the Lord are sure and altogether righteous.
They are more precious than gold, than much pure gold;
they are sweeter than honey, than honey from the comb.
Eat honey, my son, for it is good;
honey from the comb is sweet to your taste.
Psalm 19:9b–10, Proverbs 24:13

Abraham's faith in God was further demonstrated when he gave his nephew, Lot, first opportunity to choose where to live (Genesis 13:8–9). Abraham had full confidence God would bless him wherever he lived. Faith in God's goodness was the indisputable source of Abraham's wealth. But this treasure could neither be carried in a man's hand nor packed on a camel's back. It could, however, be safely hidden in a heart. And that's just where Abraham kept this treasure, taking it with him wherever God led him.

By faith Abraham,
when called to go to a place he would later receive as his *<u>inheritance</u>,*
obeyed and went,
even though he did not know here he was going.
By faith Abraham made his home in the promised land
like a stranger in a foreign country; he lived in tents, as did Isaac and Jacob,
who were heirs with him of the same promise.
Hebrews 11:8–9

<u>Inheritance</u>: Greek, *kleronomia* (klay-ron-om-eh′-o): heirship, a patrimony or possession; a possessor, a sharer by lot, i.e. an inheritor

Faith paved the way to Abraham's inheritance. By faith, Abraham went. It was faith that gave Abraham the strength to persevere when he felt alone while living in tents like a stranger in a foreign country. And it was faith which led Abraham to fulfill his oath to God concerning the spoils of the victory of Sodom.

The king of Sodom said to Abram,
"Give me the people and keep the goods for yourself."
But Abram said to the king of Sodom,
"I have raised my hand to the Lord, God Most High, Creator of heaven and earth,
and have taken an oath that I will accept nothing belonging to you,
not even a thread or the thong of a sandal, so that you will never be able to say,
'I made Abram rich.' "
Genesis 14:21–23

"Hey, Abraham, here's you some extra money," the King of Sodom offers. "No," was Abraham's answer. "I won't keep it. I've made an oath to God, and if I become a wealthy man, it will be from the hand of God, not you."

In Abraham's mind, if he'd taken wealth from the spoils of this victory, he would have been guilty of stealing. Stealing? "But the king of Sodom *offered* the goods of the victory to Abraham. How could this be stealing?" The words of Abraham are self explanatory: ". . . so that you will never be able to say, 'I made Abram rich.' " Abraham believed if he'd taken goods from the King of Sodom, he would have robbed God of the credit for making him a rich man. It's clear Abraham never wanted it said that Sodom (the epitome of lust and greed) was the source of his wealth.

You may say to yourself,
"My power and the strength of my hands have produced this wealth for me."
But remember the Lord your God,
for it is he who gives you the ability to produce wealth,
and so confirms his covenant, which he swore to your forefathers, as it is today.
Deuteronomy 8:17–18

It's easy to forget that God is the One who give us the ability to work and produce wealth. Actually, everything we own belonged to God before it was given to us. That thought bears repeating. *Our possessions belonged to God before they belonged to us.* It's much easier to return wealth to its rightful owner when we understand that, much like a gift belongs to the giver before it's given to the recipient, so our wealth belonged to God before it was entrusted to us.

SECURITY BLANKET

"Mama, I know you love me 'cause you put an extra blanket on me last night."
John Menser, Feb. 22, 1990

"You shall not steal."
Exodus 20:15

Steal: Hebrew, *ganab* (gaw-nab'): to thieve, to deceive, to get by stealth (secret, underhanded procedure)

What stimulates a person to steal? We might understand the motives of the person who steals in order to feed himself or his family. But why would a man whose belly is full and whose needs are met feel compelled to steal? Lot, do you have another lesson to teach us?

This is the account of Terah.
Terah became the father of Abram, Nahor and Haran.
And Haran became the father of Lot.
While his father Terah was still alive,
Haran died in Ur of the Chaldeans, in the land of his birth.
Terah took his son Abram, his grandson Lot son of Haran,
and his daughter-in-law Sarai, the wife of his son Abram,
and together they set out from Ur of the Chaldeans to go to Canaan.
But when they came to Haran, they settled there.
Genesis 11:27-28, 31 (emphasis mine)

The bottom line is this: Lot had Grandfather Terah and Uncle Abraham to rely on and, no doubt, he'd be well taken care of; but a grandpa and an uncle can't take the place of a father. And Lot's father was gone.

Scripture tells us God blessed Lot with an abundance of flocks, herds and tents (Genesis 13:5). Who can question that, materially speaking, Lot was a rich man? But what about Lot's emotional coffer, how full was it? Could it be there's another reason why Lot chose to live in Sodom?

Perhaps within the well-watered plains of Sodom Lot saw a secure future for his family, and, emotionally speaking, security was something Lot might have lost when his father died. Could it be that, when Lot surveyed the land near Sodom and then compared it to the land of Hebron, he made his choice based on a need for security rather than on faith in God?

Lot's life may prove to be a mystery for us. It will leave us wondering how two men (Lot and Abraham) coming from the same family (Terah's) could live such different lives: one pitching his tents near Sodom, a city renowned for sin, the other living in Canaan where he built an altar to God under the great trees of Mamre (Genesis 14:12–13, 18).

Lot likely thought he was taking good care of himself and his family by choosing the well-watered plains of Jordan, working hard, and watching his wealth increase.

Then came the judgment of God.

By the time Lot reached Zoar, the sun had risen over the land.
Then the Lord rained down burning sulfur on Sodom and Gomorrah–from the Lord out of the heavens. Early the next morning Abraham got up and returned to the place where he had stood before the Lord. He looked down toward Sodom and Gomorrah, toward all the land of the plain, and he saw dense smoke rising from the land, like smoke from a furnace.
Genesis 19:23–24, 27–28

Lot looked at smoke and ashes and death and *Lot is not there.* Why?

So when God destroyed the cities of the plain,
he remembered Abraham,
and he brought Lot out of the catastrophe that overthrew the cities where Lot had lived.
Genesis 19:29 (emphasis mine)

What was Uncle Abraham doing while God's judgment was consuming Lot's wealth?

And the Lord said, "Shall I hide from Abraham what I am doing,
since Abraham shall surely become a great and mighty nation,
and all the nations of the earth shall be blessed in him?
For I have known him,
in order that he may command his children and his household after him,
that they keep the way of the Lord, to do righteousness and justice,
that the Lord may bring to Abraham what He has spoken to him."
Genesis 18:17–19 (NKJV)

Command: Hebrew, *tsavah* (tsaw-vaw´): to constitute, to enjoin, to appoint, to bid, to charge, to put or set in order
Keep: Hebrew, *shamar* (shaw-mar'): to take heed, to look narrowly, to beware, to keep the mark, to observe, to preserve, to wait, to hedge about (as with thorns), to watch, to protect, to guard

Higher Calling

by Pat Menser

(Inspired by a little boy named Adam. I remember your freckles and red curly hair.)

(*Proverbs* 22:6, *Galatians* 6:9)

No, it didn't come to me in a vision
Or a loud voice piercing the night.
No one knocked at my door and said, "Enter."
There were no bright shining, radiant lights.

But when seeking His will for this mother
I stood quietly waiting His call.
He gently answered my questions and doubting
Saying, "Give me your life. That is all."

For your place is not out in the missions
Or feeding the hungry and poor.
It won't appear as a noble position
But the rewards will be greater by far.

I want you to nurture your children
To guide them and teach them My ways
So that when they are older and tempted
They'll rest in My Word and not sway.

For I see that My children are dying
For lack of guidance and care.
They come home to their house or apartment
To find that no one is there.

So take honor in being a mother.
Take pride in cooking their meals.
Lift high the name of their father.
I'll help you wipe up one more spill.

For when you take care of My children
And put your desires to the side
You'll see them mature in the ways of the Lord
And in their hearts know that I will abide.

Train up a child in the way he should go,
And when he is old he will not depart from it.
And let us not grow weary while doing good,
for in due season we shall reap if we do not lose heart.
Proverbs 22:6, Galatians 6:9 (NKJV)

After the destruction of Sodom and Gomorrah,

Lot and his two daughters left Zoar and settled in the mountains,
for he was afraid to stay in Zoar. He and his two daughters lived in a cave.
One day the older daughter said to the younger, "Our father is old,
and there is no man around here to lie with us, as is the custom all over the earth.
Let's get our father to drink wine and then lie with him
and preserve our family line through our father."
Genesis 19:30–32

Of course it was an awful thing to do, but what kind of example had Lot set for his daughters? He'd placed them near a city notorious for lust and greed. Perhaps these young girls were in the next room and overheard their father offering their virgin bodies to the lustful demands of the men of Sodom. We understand Eastern hospitality demanded much of its host, but nevertheless and regardless of custom, Lot's daughters were surely wounded by their father's offer to give them over for the sexual pleasure of the entire city!

Before they had gone to bed,
all the men from every part of the city of Sodom–
both young and old–surrounded the house.
They called to Lot, "Where are the men who came to you tonight?
Bring them out to us so that we can have sex with them."
Lot went outside to meet them and shut the door behind him and said,
"No, my friends. Don't do this wicked thing.
Look, I have two daughters who have never slept with a man.
Let me bring them out to you, and you can do what you like with them.
But don't do anything to these men,
for they have come under the protection of my roof,"
Genesis 19:4–8 (emphasis mine)

We see Lot offering his daughters' virgin bodies to sex-thirsty men. Later in Lot's relationship with his daughters, there will be acts of deception and incest, all of which will leave us wondering how Lot's daughters truly felt about their father (Genesis 19:30-31). These behaviors draw a sharp distinction between Lot as a parent and Abraham, who is commanding his family to do righteousness and justice. Is it possible Lot withheld from his daughters the very possession he was denied by the death of his father: that of a father's love and training in the ways of the Lord?

If this is true, then it is also very sad. One wonders where Lot got so "off track." Perhaps he spent too much time with his friends at the gateway of the city. Maybe Lot was preoccupied with the sights and sounds of Sodom. Perhaps it's simply that Abraham enjoyed spending time with God while Lot did not. You'll recall that, when Sodom was destroyed, Lot's life was spared, not because of Lot's prayers or petitions but because God *remembered Abraham* (Genesis 19:29).

Parents, we're stealing from our children and we don't even know it. We're robbing them by giving them Sodom instead of sharing the deep friendship they can have with God. Abraham was a wealthy man, wealthier than Lot for that matter. The difference is that, though Abraham lived in a land of plenty, the plenty didn't own him. Abraham loved God and taught his children to do the same. And it's from this perspective, one of relationship, faith and obedience, that God blessed Abraham to become the father of many nations.

DON'T BREAK MY HEART

Clearly, stealing is wrong on any level. I believe that when a person breaks God's commandment, "Do not steal," that person is really saying, "God, I'm afraid. I don't know you very well. I don't have a relationship with you that gives me assurance you'll meet my needs." It's not so much about breaking a commandment as it is about breaking a heart, the heart of a Father who longs to be known as our Provider.

I've been robbed before, by a close friend. But it wasn't the theft that broke my heart–it was the lack of trust this person had in me. All he had to do was ask for what he took, and I would have gladly given it to him.

Was he afraid to ask? Did he not want me to know about his need? It *broke my heart* that he didn't know everything I owned was his, just for the asking. If someone has stolen from us, God's Word commands we leave room for *his* judgment, a judgment which may well include mercy.

Do not take revenge, my friends, but leave room for God's wrath,
for it is written: "It is mine to avenge; I will repay," says the Lord.
On the contrary: "If your enemy is hungry, feed him;
if he is thirsty, give him something to drink.
In doing this, you will heap burning coals on his head."
Do not be overcome by evil, but overcome evil with good.
Romans 12:19–21

In the days before matches and access to fire, heaping burning coals on a person's head was a gesture of generosity. It was a good thing to do, as you were giving him the ability to be warm and sustain life. If someone steals from you, don't avenge. Overcome evil with good.

LOT, RIGHTEOUS?

"Mama, the reason I like parents so much is they make you feel safe and they protect you." John Menser, Feb. 6, 1990

Lot didn't have that as a young boy: a parent who made him feel safe and protected. Remember, Lot's father died, placing Lot under the care of his grandfather. Let Lot's life be a warning to us. Before we make decisions as to where to live, whom to marry, or the vocation to pursue, let's first examine our motives behind these important decisions. Of course we should be mindful of our past, but let's not allow voids in our lives to dictate future decisions. For if we make choices based primarily on the need to compensate for what we don't have, we may be putting ourselves in a position that leaves us vulnerable to greed and struggling to maintain intimate fellowship with God.

For the love of money is a root of all kinds of evil.
Some people, eager for money, have wandered from the faith
and pierced themselves with many griefs.
1 Timothy 6:10

I believe Lot wandered. He chose to live in a land renowned for greed and sexual immorality. As a result of this decision, Lot's wealth went up in smoke, he was prone to drunkenness, and he was deceived by his daughters.

Let's learn from Lot's mistakes. Greed, dependence on others for spiritual strength, drunkenness, and incest all shade the character and reputation of Lot. His life appears to be one of utter defeat. Yet with all the lessons Lot has taught us, his final lesson may be the most difficult to understand.

. . . if he condemned the cities of Sodom and Gomorrah by burning them to ashes,
and made them an example of what is going to happen to the ungodly;
and if he rescued Lot, a righteous man,
who was distressed by the filthy lives of lawless men
(for that righteous man, living among them day after day,
was tormented in his righteous soul by the lawless deeds he saw and heard)–
if this is so, then the Lord knows how to rescue godly men from trials–
and hold the unrighteous for the day of judgment.
2 Peter 2:6–9 (emphases mine)

How could a man like Lot be described as "righteous and godly"? At first glance this New Testament description of Lot seems totally out of character; yet it makes perfect sense when read under the light of God's grace. For it is here, in the life of a man named Lot, where we see the faithfulness–not of Lot but of God.

In all fairness to Lot, let's consider the possibility that God had reasons for allowing him to choose the "well-watered plains of Jordan," thus positioning Abraham to settle in the land of Canaan. To us it may appear as greed on the part of Lot, but God might have seen it differently. And perhaps, rather than allow harm to come to his visiting angels, Lot thought it noble and culturally correct to offer his daughters to the sex-thirsty demands of the homosexual community. Another possibility is that Lot was so well acquainted with these men and their sexual appetites that he really didn't think his offer would be accepted. After all, the men of Sodom were wanting sex with angels whom they thought were *men*

(Genesis 19:5). We might see Lot offering his daughters' virgin bodies to these men as unthinkable, but God's vantage point and his purposes are always higher than ours.

In order to have even partial insight into God's opinion of Lot, we need to acknowledge our disadvantage. Our desire to uncover the truth, even our fervent study of Scripture, leaves us lacking in our understanding of Lot compared to God's understanding of him. Our eyes easily observe the shortcomings in Lot's life; and while his moral failures flash brilliantly before us, his goodness may remain hidden. God's vision, however, pierces deeply into the heart of this seemingly backslidden man, and perhaps it was there, in the depths of this man's heart, where God saw Lot tormented by the sinful behavior of Sodom (2 Peter 2:6–9).

What an opportunity we have to learn from the life of Lot. How torturous it must have been for a man such as he to witness the sins of Sodom. Harassed by day and needled by night, Lot was a righteous man living in an oppressive environment. But the true marvel of Lot's story is that, even though his outward behavior didn't appear to reflect righteousness, God judged Lot by what he saw in his heart and, according to Scripture, God saw a tormented man.

The life of Lot supports the truth that once a person is made righteous in God's eyes, he remains so regardless of his faults and failures. This doesn't mean Lot or his family would escape the painful consequences of Lot's choices. It does mean, however, that, due to *God's* faithfulness, Lot maintained his righteous standing with God.

For though a righteous man falls seven times, he rises again,
but the wicked are brought down by calamity.
Proverbs 24:16

Wicked men fall and are brought *down* by calamity. Righteous men fall and *rise* again. We need to give Lot credit for at least trying to lead his family out of Sodom when destruction was imminent. It's a small but significant observation to make, however, that when Lot's sons-in-law heard Lot's warning, they thought he was joking (Genesis 19:14-16). And did you notice that when the angels told Lot to leave Sodom, he hesitated, and the angels literally had to grab the hands of Lot, his wife and two daughters? Rather than witnessing hesitation from Lot, wouldn't it be encouraging to have seen decisive strength and leadership flowing from the patriarch of this family? Somehow Lot just doesn't seem to demand the respect one would expect, especially when one considers that his desire to lead his family to safety was received with such uncertainty.

Abraham, on the other hand, was a decisive father who was confident in his ability to lead his family in the ways of the Lord. Abraham didn't question God. Time and again Scripture reveals Abraham's relationship with God as one of *immediate obedience*. Indeed, the predominant way Abraham imparted wealth to his children was by living a life of unswerving obedience to God. I believe the reason Isaac was so compliant to his father's request to be sacrificed to God was that Isaac had seen his father live a life wholly devoted to his own Father (Genesis 22:1–9).

Fix these words of mine in your hearts and minds;
tie them as symbols on your hands and bind them on your foreheads.
Teach them to your children,
talking about them when you sit at home and when you walk along the road,
when you lie down and when you get up.
Write them on the door frames of your houses and on your gates. . .
Deuteronomy 11:18–20

Years earlier in the Valley of Shaveh, we saw Abraham's integrity when he tithed his resources to Melchizedek. Throughout his life, Abraham is seen being generous with his nephew and sharing his wealth with his children—not his money, not his cattle or land, but something far greater: *his friendship with and obedience to God* (James 2:23). Here, from the very wellspring of their father's wealth, Abraham's children could drink and be refreshed.

DELIGHT

"Everyone who drinks this water will be thirsty again,
but whoever drinks the water I (Jesus) give him will never thirst.
Indeed the water I give him will become in him
a spring of water welling up to eternal life."
John 4:1

Do Not Steal

PRINCIPLES

1. A believer's life should include expressions of faith.

2. God rewards those who earnestly seek him.

3. God expects his children to live by faith and to persevere in doing his will.

4. The desire to be rich can cause us to wander from God and from his will for our lives.

5. The desire to be rich can lead to many griefs and regrets.

6. People who know God's love feel wealthy and satisfied.

7. God is faithful even when we're not.

8. It's vital that parents share their relationship with God with their children.

9. The more we know God, the more faith we'll have in him to provide for our needs.

Do Not Steal

DISCUSSION QUESTIONS

1. Proverbs 8:18 tells us "With God are riches and honor, enduring wealth and prosperity." What does it mean to be rich with honor and have enduring wealth?

2. Who gives us the ability to produce wealth? (Deuteronomy 8:17–18a)

3. Correlate possessing faith in God with not stealing from God.

4. Can you identify some possible deficits in Lot's life which may have fed his desire to live near Sodom?

5. What does the love of money have the power to do to a person?

6. Why is money not the root of evil, but the *love of money* is?

7. What does it mean to "wander from the faith"?

8. In today's society, what does it look like to command our children in the way of the Lord?

9. Compare the level of respect Lot's daughters had for him with the respect Isaac demonstrated toward his father, Abraham.

10. What is a modern-day comparison of "heaping coals of fire upon a person's head"?

What you have said in the dark will be heard in the daylight . . .

Luke 12:3a

Chapter 9

Do Not Bear False Witness

Exodus 20:16

"Deception Will Deceive You."

In this chapter you will read about:

- behaviors indicative of sin in our lives;
- actions David took in response to his sin;
- the purpose and power of the tongue;
- how the "the fear of the Lord" leads to wisdom and truth;
- the definition of a hypocrite.

Hebrew/Greek word studies: subtle/crafty, false, witness, justified, condemned, deceit, hypocrisy, double-minded, unstable

"He (the devil) was a murderer from the beginning,
not holding to the truth, for there is no truth in him.
When he lies, he speaks his native language,
for he is a liar and the father of lies."
John 8:44b

This chapter exposes tactics the devil uses to draw us away from God. We'll see how our tendency to blame others for our sins causes us to fall short of true repentance, and we'll come to understand the importance of fearing God and hiding his word in our heart in order to know when deception is near.

We'll look into the heart of God and try to understand how he felt when Adam and Eve hid from him. And we'll marvel at how God's love endures beyond even his judgment.

The way it might have been:

"It's a viper!" exclaimed Isaac.

"Be still, my son. His eye is keen, watching our every movement."

"May I speak?" Isaac asked.

"Not now, Isaac. The serpent watches even the movement of our lips. Carefully, with the grace of a doe, move slowly away from its sight," instructed Abraham.

The terror of the day was still with young Isaac, even as the sun was setting behind his tent.

"Father, I saw it," said Isaac.

"You mean, the serpent?"

"That, and . . ."

"Speak freely, my son."

"In your eyes . . . I saw . . . *fear*," replied Isaac.

"And it frightened you?" asked Abraham.

"I thought you would confront the serpent and dare it never to cross our path again. But instead of fighting, you retreated," said Isaac, "and I am bewildered."

There was silence between father and son. Abraham knew his words must be well-chosen.

"For years I have watched the way of the serpent. He is a beautiful creature, but his beauty is deceptive," said Abraham. "Many times I've seen the serpent lie in wait for his next meal. He appears to be sleeping, coiled and unconcerned. Then, with the speed of lightning, he lashes toward his prey, reveals his forked tongue, and mercilessly sinks his fangs deep into his victim. And, as if his bite and poison were not enough, his method of destroying his meal is even worse."

"What do you mean?" asked Isaac.

"It's the way he eats his victim. His jaws detach from their sockets, allowing the snake to swallow his meal whole. It is within the belly of the serpent where his victim is crushed, chewed and finally dissolved," explained Abraham.

"Is that why he frightened you?" asked Isaac.

"Not exactly, my son. It's difficult to explain. Let's ask Jehovah to give understanding in the 'ways of the serpent.' "

CUNNING AND CLEVER

Now the serpent was more subtle than any beast of the field which the Lord God had made.
Genesis 3:1a (KJV)

Subtle: Hebrew, *aruwn* (aw-room ′): cunning in a bad sense (through the idea of smoothness), crafty

"Isaac, do you know the meaning of 'subtle'?" asked Abraham.

"Not really," confessed Isaac.

"It means the serpent is a most clever beast. He appears beautiful, but beneath his beauty lives a very cunning creature. He's a master at captivating men with his charm. And once he has our attention, we become vulnerable to his venom," Abraham explained.

"What's in his venom?" asked Isaac. "Why is it so deadly?"

He (Satan) said to the woman,
"Did God really say, 'You must not eat from any tree in the garden'?"
Genesis 3:1b (emphasis mine)

"Notice, my son, what the serpent said to the woman: 'Did God *really* say?' The serpent's most cunning venom is that of planting doubt in the minds of men. He does this by cleverly mixing his lies with God's truth, resulting in an almost imperceptible poison so deadly even the wisest of men can fail to detect its danger. I warn you, Isaac," Abraham said sternly, "The serpent is the master of deception."

"But, Father," Isaac pleaded, "it brings such pleasure to look upon his beauty, his stripes, the colors and patterns of his skin . . ."

"Stop! Stop!" Abraham interrupted. "Now even my own son is being lured by his charm! I will listen no more; you are the one to listen now. My words will protect you from many dangers lying in wait for you. Listen, my son, listen to your father."

"I know the serpent is appealing to the eye. I even know his present beauty pales in comparison to his former state," said Abraham.

"What do you mean, 'former state'?" asked Isaac.

"Isaac, at one time the serpent walked upright. And because it was a serpent who brought deception to the world, Jehovah said:

'Cursed are you above all the livestock and all the wild animals!
You will crawl on your belly and you will eat dust all the days of your life.' "
Genesis 3:14b

"A serpent—with *legs?*" asked Isaac.

"It's believed so," Abraham answered. "And Isaac, the beauty you see now is a shadow of the beauty he once possessed. Can you imagine that?"

"Oh, Father, it surpasses my understanding."

"Isaac, my son, I do not fear the serpent, but I do possess knowledge of his insidious ways. Many times this knowledge has prevented me from coming near to him or even crossing his path. Without an understanding of the ways of the serpent, I would have, long ago, fallen prey to his venom," said Abraham.

"So, you weren't afraid of him?" asked Isaac. "It wasn't fear I saw in your eyes?"

"No, my son, it was not fear. It was knowledge," Abraham replied.

WILL—WILL NOT

And the Lord God commanded the man,
"You are free to eat from any tree in the garden;
but you must not eat from the tree of the knowledge of good and evil,
for when you eat of it you will surely die."
Genesis 2:16–17

The Lord gave Adam two specific instructions concerning the garden:

- he could: eat from any tree;
- he could not: eat from the tree of the knowledge of good and evil.

That's it. Those were his instructions.

Then the serpent came to the woman and questioned the word of God.

"Did God really say, 'You must not eat from any tree in the garden'?"
Genesis 3:1b

This is how Eve answered him:

"We may eat fruit from the trees in the garden,
but God did say,
'You must not eat fruit from the tree that is in the middle of the garden,
and you must not touch it, or you will die.' "
Genesis 3:2–3 (emphasis mine)

Eve is taking his bait. The moment she begins to question God's words, she distorts them. It's a subtle change. Did you catch it?

"*And you must not touch it.*" God didn't say that. God never told Adam and Eve not to touch the tree. He told Adam not to eat fruit from that tree, but God said nothing about touching it. Eve is insinuating that God was asking way too much of her (*poor me, I can't even touch it*). Such reasoning puts God at fault for being overly demanding in the first place. See how subtle this serpent can be?

Satan has Eve just where he wants her: *willing to distort the words of God.* He continues his conniving plan by telling Eve she will "be like God, knowing good and evil," if she eats from the tree. He even goes so far as to tell her that eating from this tree is good for her body, pleasing to the eye, and that she would gain knowledge (Genesis 3:6a). His enticement can be heard in the words:

"You will not surely die," the serpent said to the woman.
Genesis 3:4a (emphasis mine)

Satan told Eve: "You will not surely die."

But God had already told Adam: "You will surely die."

But you must not eat from the tree of the knowledge of good and evil,
for when you eat of it you will surely die.
Genesis 2:17b (emphasis mine)

"Will not" is what our flesh wants to hear. Go *ahead, you will not . . . Do that, you will not . . . Don't worry about it, you will not . . .*

NAKED. AFRAID. HIDING

Then the eyes of both of them were opened, and they realized they were naked; so they sewed fig leaves together and made coverings for themselves.
Genesis 3:6-7 (emphasis mine)

Having three grandchildren, ages four and under, we see a lot of naked little bodies running around our house. They scamper away before we can dress them, and they undress before we can catch them. Each one delights when it's "bubble-time" and they get to jump in the tub with rubber duckies, boats, foam toys that stick to the tile, and squirt bottles used to conquer invading pirates. Oh, how I'll miss these years of innocence and the joy of their unabashed nakedness. All too soon they will realize they're naked, and that's when I'll know their innocence is gone. The same can be said of God. When Adam and Eve realized they were naked, God knew they'd lost their innocence.

Then the man and his wife heard the sound of the Lord God
as he was walking in the garden in the cool of the day,
and they hid from the Lord God among the trees of the garden.
But the Lord God called to the man, "Where are you?"
He answered, "I heard you in the garden,
and I was afraid because I was naked; so I hid.
And he (God) said, "Who told you that you were naked?
Have you eaten from the tree that I commanded you not to eat from?"
Genesis 3:8–11 (emphasis mine)

Adam was afraid to be in the presence of his Father who, just a short time earlier, had been walking alongside Adam in the beautiful Garden of Eden. This was a Father who had created the earth, sun, moon and stars for Adam, the earth to walk upon and the plants to feast upon. This was a Father who took a bone from Adam's side and created a beautiful companion for him. And so we see a shamed and guilty Adam, afraid and hiding from his all-knowing, all-providing God. But Adam couldn't hide for long. Soon the voice of God was calling:

"Where are you?"
Genesis 3:9b

Unable to run from the voice God, Adam was forced to face his Creator. It was then when Adam chose to add yet another sin to the one he'd just committed: for rather than own up to rebelling against God, Adam chose to argue his case to God, thinking he could somehow justify his rebellious behavior.

The man said, "The woman you put here with me–
she gave me some fruit from the tree, and I ate it."
Genesis 3:12 (emphasis mine)

1. woman
2. you (God)

Don't blame me! You're the one who put the woman here. Blaming someone else for our sin is our first, almost knee-jerk response. But Adam didn't play the "blame game" alone. Seeing that her husband was more than willing to hold her responsible for their dilemma, Eve quickly thought of the perfect place where she could unload her responsibility for their behavior.

Then the Lord God said to the woman,
"What is this you have done?"
The woman said, "The serpent deceived me, and I ate."
Genesis 3:13

Don't blame me. Blame the snake. If Adam wouldn't shoulder the responsibility for his rebellion, and if Eve was unwilling to share in the blame, then the next best option was to point to the serpent. Forget that Adam and Eve were creatures of free will; abandon the thought that God had given them specific instructions concerning this tree. Adam and Eve didn't want to be reminded of these facts. Their energies were focused on salvaging their reputations, which, it appears, was more important than maintaining their fellowship with God.

Perhaps Adam and Eve thought that partial repentance was enough to reestablish their relationship with God. However, the truth is: there's no such thing as partial repentance. The very definition of repentance defies the inclusion of "partial."

For godly sorrow produces repentance leading to salvation, not to be regretted; but the sorrow of the world produces death.
2 Corinthians 7:10 (NKJV)

Repentance: Greek, *metanoia* (met-an´-oy-ah): reformation, reversal; to think differently, to reconsider

The secular definition of *repentance* is "to feel sorry, self-reproachful or contrite for a past action, to feel remorse, sorrow or regret." If we're looking for forgiveness from the world, then the secular definition might do. God's definition of *repentance*, however, goes much deeper. From God's perspective, true repentance occurs when you think differently afterwards, when there's been a reversal and reformation in your attitude toward your behavior. The purpose of repentance is to have both a changed mind and changed behavior.

Adam admitted his sin to God, but he did so with excuses attached to his confession. Here we see a husband's "partial" admission of fault, placing the blame on his wife and on God for giving him that wife. Strange that, just moments earlier, Adam was a devoted husband, willing to do anything his wife asked of him—even disobey his Father. Now, with his sin clearly exposed, loyalty to his spouse is nowhere to be found. Sin has always had power to divide even the closest relationships.

Eve's confession is equally superficial. Compare her words, "The serpent deceived me" (Genesis 13:13b), to the words spoken by King David when he sinned against the Lord:

Blessed is he whose transgressions are forgiven, whose sins are covered.
Blessed is the man whose sin the Lord does not count against him
and in whose spirit is not deceit.
When I kept silent, my bones wasted away through my groaning all day long.
For day and night your hand was heavy upon me;
my strength was sapped as in the heat of the summer.
Then I acknowledged my sin to you and did not cover up my iniquity.
I said, "I will confess my transgressions to the Lord"---and you forgave the guilt of my sins.
Psalm 32:1–5 (emphases mine)

1. David acknowledged his sin.
2. David did not cover up his sin.
3. David confessed his sin.

And compare to Peter's response when he realized he'd denied the Lord:

And he went outside and wept bitterly.
Luke 22:62

Do we hear the same brokenness in Eve's voice that we heard in David's and Peter's? Was there godly sorrow in her confession, or was she merely saddened that her sin couldn't be hidden? One can interpret Eve's words from several perspectives. Perhaps it would help to hear her confession again.

The woman said,
"The serpent deceived me, and I ate."
Genesis 3:13b

Imagine the scene: man, God's greatest creation, has just fallen prey to sin. Not long ago God had opened his mouth and tenderly breathed life into the nostrils of Adam. Now God's first-born has disobeyed the singular command God had given him. Was it too much to require that Adam not eat from one tree, just one? After all, the bounty of the entire Garden was given to Adam and his wife, with only one exception. Could this Father have been any more generous?

God was quite capable of finding an excuse for his children's rebellion, if one had existed. Their behavior, however, couldn't be traced to an unhealthy childhood, nor was it hunger that drove them to the tree. There were no parents to blame, no bad marriage, no lost job. Oh, how painful it must have been for God to absorb the blow that his children had willfully disobeyed him, particularly when he'd been so clear in revealing his will to them.

HEARTBROKEN

For the next few moments let's try to understand the heart of God as he experienced sin in the lives of His children. Let's look for that place, the point of Adam and Eve's disobedience, that brought God the most pain. Was it that his children drew near to the serpent, spent time with him and entertained his voice? Was God hurting because they'd compromised what he said to them in order to justify their desires? Or was it the fact that Adam gave more heed to the words of his wife than to those spoken by God? Might God's most intense pain have been their ingratitude for his lush provisions in the Garden of Eden? These were, undoubtedly, all sources of sorrow for our Lord. But the question we're looking to answer is this: Was there a singular reason, one which stood above all others, that obligated a loving Father to speak these words to his children?

To the woman he said, "I will greatly increase your pains in childbearing;
with pain you will give birth to children.
Your desire will be for your husband, and he will rule over you."
To Adam he said, "Because you listened to your wife and ate from the tree about which I commanded you, 'You must not eat of it,' cursed is the ground because of you;
through painful toil you will eat of it all the days of your life.
It will produce thorns and thistles for you, and you will eat the plants of the field.
By the sweat of your brow you will eat your food
until you return to the ground, since from it you were taken;
for dust you are and to dust you will return."
Genesis 3:16–19

What was God feeling when sin entered the lives of His children? Remember, this was the first family ever to sin against the Lord. It was the first household ever to fall prey to the "ways of the serpent." And it was the first time God's eyes looked upon children, created in *his* image, lured by the serpent's charm, guilty and ashamed of their sin, hiding from their Father while justifying their actions.

It was a pitiful sight. Let's listen closely to the question God had earlier asked Adam. Perhaps we'll hear something.

"Where are you?"
Genesis 3:9b

Do you hear it–the heart of a Father, breaking? It's as though God is saying, "Adam, I miss you. I'm lonely for your fellowship. Before you sinned against my command, we were inseparable. Where are you, my precious child?"

The sad reality is that Adam and Eve didn't seem to realize the anguish they'd caused their Father. Perhaps they were in such pain themselves that it was difficult to feel for another. It's likely they were so ashamed that they thought God wouldn't want fellowship with them any longer. And so they reasoned that hiding from the Person they'd wounded was the only thing they could do.

They were so wrong. Because of their shame and guilt, they didn't hear the heart of God's question. They were too busy hiding from God to be able to feel his love for them. This is what shame does: it keeps us from receiving love from our Father.

Yes, sin has consequences. God's holiness demanded that Adam and Eve leave his garden. Their behavior prevented them from enjoying a relationship with God that, at one time, was innocent, open and trusting. How true it is that intimacy is compromised when deception enters a relationship. Mercifully, however, God's duty to judge does not negate his ability to love. Notice also that God did not leave his children naked.

The Lord God made garments of skin for Adam and his wife and clothed them.
Genesis 3:21 (emphasis mine)

To make a garment of skin an animal had to die. Blood had to be shed. Scripture doesn't say what kind of animal gave his life to cover the sins of Adam and Eve, but I'll bet it was a lamb, foreshadowing the Lamb who was to come.

. . . and without the shedding of blood there is no forgiveness.
Hebrews 9:22b

God the Father set this example for us: we have to judge the behavior of our children, and they have to experience the consequences of their choices, particularly so if they disobey a command we've clearly stated.

Our children will try to hide and blame others for their choices and, like God, it will break our hearts to dispense judgment, but we must follow through, knowing that our love for them will not only endures our discipline but far exceed it.

We still haven't answered the question: What hurt God the most when Adam and Eve sinned and then tried to deceive him by blaming others? As a parent of two grown sons, I believe what hurt God the most was that his children ran away from him with their sin, rather than toward him. How deceived we are when we forget God's deepest hurt lies in the inability of his children to *remember his goodness* more than in their ability to disobey one of his commands. Wouldn't it have been refreshing if, instead of running from God, Adam and Eve had run toward him, quickly, and sought his help concerning their sin. Just imagine if the following conversation had taken place:

"Oh, Eve, we have sinned greatly against the Lord," cried Adam.

"No," said Eve. "It is I who ate first of the tree of the knowledge of good and evil. If only I hadn't listened to—"

"We are both guilty," Adam interrupted. "Shame lies heavy upon us. We must find our Creator and confess our wickedness."

"Yes, yes, my husband. You are wise to remember the goodness of our Father. We must place our sin into the arms of his love. His judgment will be fair. Run Adam! Run quickly and find our Lord!"

A FALSE WITNESS

Who "bore false witness" to Adam and Eve about the character of God? Whose lie robbed them of their intended life in the Garden of Eden? His name is Satan, and he is the father of every lie from the time of Adam until today (John 8:44).

I recently read a story about large elephants held in captivity by small stakes hammered into the ground. It seemed odd that such powerful creatures were controlled by sticks which could have easily been broken. Apparently someone asked how this could be. "Oh, that's easy. We just tie them to the stakes when they're young. When they learn they can't get loose at a young age, they never try again."

It's time to try again. It's time to let go of the lies we've believed and the sins we've committed. It's time to experience the great love our Father has for us. It's time to live in the truth that, in Christ, we're big and powerful people! Have we forgotten the depth of our Father's love? Have we forgotten Christ wants us to live in freedom? We need to hear the truth, and the truth is that some of the things we were told when we were young *were not true*—we just believed them because we were little and bigger people said them to us.

So, before we define the meaning of a lie and a false witness, let's be aware of two things:

1. We can bear false witness to others.
2. Others can advertently or *inadvertently* bear false witness to us.

God tells us that the devil is not only a liar, but the father of all lies. In other words, all lies have their origin in the belly of a snake. The following scripture bears repeating:

"He (the devil) was a murderer from the beginning,
not holding to the truth, for there is no truth in him.
When he lies, he speaks his native language,
for he is a liar and the father of lies."
John 8:44b

For most people, examining a serpent of any kind is an unpleasant task, but that's exactly what's necessary if we're to know this reptile and understand his ways. Do you have the courage to use both hands and grab hold of this serpent, handle him and turn him over? If you do, you'll notice his underside is marked with:

Deception: misleading, cheating, trickery, defrauding and betrayal
Trickery: the use or practice of tricks, schemes or surprises in order to attain a goal or to gain an advantage over an adversary
Guile: cunning, artful deception

There are two types of liars who need to be exposed. The first type of liar knows when he lies; he takes pride in and even brags about the skill with which he deceives another. Lying is an art to him and he takes pleasure in perfecting it. He has no conscience about bearing false witness. The second type of liar doesn't take pride in his lying because he doesn't believe he's lying. This type of liar hides from the painful truth that his lifestyle is one of half-truths and crafty deception. Bearing false witness has become such a natural, everyday way of life for him that, many times, it's difficult for him to find the lies he himself has hidden.

As children of God, we must come to the place where we want our lips free of any trace of deception. We should not want "baby lies" living in our homes any more than we would want baby snakes crawling under our carpets. Do you live in a home free from lies, or have you grown accustomed to walking around wiggling things?

A TRUE WITNESS

"You shall not bear false witness against your neighbor."
Exodus 20:16 (NKJV)

Witness: Hebrew, *ed* (ayd): testimony; a recorder; to duplicate or repeat

Have you ever had a conversation recorded without your knowledge? I have—and then later I was told my words were played for others to hear. Immediately I wondered if the entirety of our conversation had been recorded or if my words had been edited and taken out of context. Of course I felt deceived—tricked—by a person I loved and whom I thought I could trust. Why hadn't he told me he was recording our conversation? His deception hurt and, yes, I felt deeply betrayed.

For days his deception lay heavily on my heart. I loved this person. He held a special place in my heart, but now I had to deal with the truth that he hadn't been honest with me. There was nothing in our conversation that I wouldn't say to him face to face. Nonetheless, he cunningly and deliberately tricked me in order to serve his own purposes.

I was unnerved, confused, and angry but also grieving at the loss of trust his scheme had produced. I began to wonder if he'd lied to me concerning other issues. Eventually, I came to realize that dwelling on his betrayal was interfering with my daily life and that I had to move on. There were goals needing to be met, one of which was to begin research of God's ninth commandment: "Thou shalt not bear false witness." As I studied this commandment, it didn't take long to realize God wanted to use the tape-recorder incident to teach me something very specific about "bearing false witness."

The dictionary defines a *witness* as "a person who sees, hears, or knows something by personal experience." He has observed an incident and can attest or give testimony to its accuracy. In a court of law, the testimony of a witness is evidence of a fact or statement.

The tape recorder incident forced a hard question on me: "Why am I obsessing about a conversation recorded on earth, while ignoring the reality that every word I've ever spoken has been witnessed and recorded in Heaven?" Ouch.

But I tell you that men will have to give account on the day of judgment
for every careless word they have spoken.
Matthew 12:36

When words are many, sin is not absent,
but he who holds his tongue is wise.
Proverbs 10:19

My dear brothers, take note of this:
Everyone should be quick to listen, slow to speak and slow to become angry. . .
James 1:19

If anyone considers himself religious and yet does not keep a tight rein on his tongue,
he deceives himself and his religion is worthless.
James 1:26

We need to slow down. At least that's what these scriptures say to me: use fewer words, be slow to speak, keep a tight rein on my tongue. (I'm envisioning a rein on my tongue like a rein on a horse. Whoa! Slow down). Oh my, there's more. . .

The tongue also is a fire, a world of evil among the parts of the body. It corrupts the whole person, sets the whole course of his life on fire, and is itself set on fire by hell.
James 3:6

"For by your words you will be justified, and by your words you will be condemned."
Matthew 12:37 (NKJV)

Justified: Greek, *dikaioo* (dik-ah-yo΄-o): to render just or innocent, to be righteous
Condemned: Greek, *katadikazo* (kat-ad-ik-ad΄-zo): to pronounce guilty, to judge against

The words we speak determine if we're in debt before God or relieved of his condemnation. Why do we use our tongues with so little thought and restraint? Why do we misrepresent the truth in even the smallest detail? What is the root of "bearing false witness"?

THE FEAR OF GOD

But the Lord God called to the man, ""Where are you?" He answered, "I heard you in the garden, and I was afraid because I was naked; so I hid."
Genesis 3:9–10

Adam and Eve didn't allow the fear of God to lead them to obey God. Following their disobedience, however, they became so afraid of God that they hid from him. It appears we can either fear God and obey him on the front end of our choices, maintaining our fellowship with him, or have no fear of God, disobey him, and fear him on the back end of our choices, making us want to hide.

Fear God—obey God's commands—remain close to God.
Don't fear God—disobey God's commands—fear God and hide.

What was lacking in Adam and Eve's lives is lacking in the lives of many of us today.

An oracle is within my heart concerning the sinfulness of the wicked:
There is no fear of God before his eyes.
For in his own eyes he flatters himself too much to detect or hate his sin.
Psalm 36:1-2

Let's be clear on what it means to "fear God."

To fear the Lord is to hate evil;
I hate pride and arrogance, evil behavior and perverse speech.
Proverbs 8:13

There are six things the Lord hates
seven that are detestable to him: . . .
Proverbs 6:16-19

Here they are:

- haughty eyes,
- a lying tongue,
- hands that shed innocent blood,
- a heart that devises wicked schemes,
- feet that are quick to rush into evil,
- a false witness who pours out lies,
- and a man who stirs up dissension among brothers.

Detestable/Abomination: Hebrew, *toebah* (to-ay-baw´): abhorrent; to loathe

Detestable, disgusting, repulsive—we all have things that turn our stomachs and send us to the bathroom. Imagine God feeling the same way when his holy eyes look upon such behaviors. But it doesn't do us any good to know what's detestable to God unless we can apply this knowledge to our lives. Here's what I see when I look at what God hates to see:

- Haughty eyes: I fear discrimination.
- A lying tongue: I fear how others would react to knowing the truth.
- Hands that shed innocent blood: I fear losing my freedom, lifestyle, reputation.
- A heart that devises wicked schemes: I fear things not turning out as I want them to.

- Feet that are quick to rush into evil: I fear the discomfort of denying myself fleshly desires.
- A false witness who pours out lies: I fear the repercussions of telling the truth.
- A man who stirs up dissension: I fear the stillness of truth, so I create chaos and confusion to keep me distracted.

All seven of the things God hates can be traced back to one word: fear—not of God, but of man.

Fear of man will prove to be a snare,
but whoever trusts in the Lord is kept safe.
Proverbs 29:25

A snare is a trap for catching game, and we're the game. Get a picture of that because snares are usually camouflaged and well-hidden. They'll catch us by surprise if we're not careful.

It's natural to seek comfort. It's natural to want to protect our reputations. It's natural to want to be accepted by our peers. And it's natural to want to avoid humiliation. But beware: for what appears to be a life-saver can quickly distance us from the Lord. It's a slow float, and the ride may even be fun at first, but holding on to our reputations can propel us downward, encouraging us to use trickery and schemes, any lie it takes in order to save face. It's an almost imperceptible spiral, and we won't like where it takes us.

Soon we'll find ourselves in a struggle, not only with bearing false witness but also with pride. Our consuming desire to protect our reputations takes on a life of itself, rolling and growing—snowballing until we find ourselves wearing our masks of hypocrisy more and more. The irony of this cycle is that, as each lie is added to our lives, we're rendered even "more blind," unable to see we're expending enormous amounts of energy just keeping our lies fed and afloat. In truth, being truthful isn't even about what comes out of our mouth but what's in our hearts.

For out of the overflow of the heart the mouth speaks.
Matthew 12:34b (emphasis mine)

Man is comprised of body, soul, and spirit. Daily we feed our flesh the nourishment it needs to remain strong and healthy. But do we ever stop to think that our spirit needs its own kind of food? Just as the mouth is the physical opening where food is received into our bodies, the eyes are the spiritual opening where nourishment enters our spirit. It's not what passes the lips of our mouths that defiles us, it's the evil that passes through the lids of our eyes going straight to our hearts.

"The eye is the lamp of the body.
If your eyes are good, your whole body will be full of light.
But if your eyes are bad, your whole body will be full of darkness."
Matthew 6:22–23a

What spiritual food are we serving in our homes? Do we slant the truth////just a little bit? Are small deceptions acceptable if they help make life a little easier? Perhaps bearing false witness isn't the main course at our family dinner table, maybe just a side dish, perhaps only a condiment. But remember, it's the *seasoned liar* who knows how to use only a little bit of salt or pepper to change the flavor of a whole meal.

Therefore, rid yourselves of all malice and all deceit,
hypocrisy, envy, and slander of every kind.
I Peter 2:1

Deceit: Greek, *dolos* (dol´-os): to decoy; a trick or bait, subtlety; crafty

Hypocrisy: Greek, *hupkrisis* (hoop-ok´-ree-sis): acting under a feigned part; deceit

"A hypocrite is described as 'one who answers as a stage-actor.' It was a custom for Greek and Roman actors to speak in large masks with mechanical devices for augmenting the force of the voice; hence the word became used metaphorically of 'a dissembler, a hypocrite' " (Vine, 316).

Bearing false witness is equated to an actor wearing a mask and pretending to be something he's not. Like an actor, the hypocrite plays the part he thinks will please his audience and earn him the loudest applause.

BECOMING A WISE PERSON

The fear of the Lord is the beginning of knowledge,
but fools despise wisdom and discipline.
Proverbs 1:7

Scripture teaches that, in order to become a wise person, we must live our lives in the fear of the Lord. So how is the fear of the Lord established in our lives? How do we "get" the fear of the Lord so necessary for obtaining wisdom and walking in truth?

Teach me your way, O Lord, and I will walk in your truth;
give me an undivided heart, that I may fear your name.
Above all else, guard your heart; for it is the wellspring of life.
Psalm 86:11, Proverbs 4:23

King David understood the importance of protecting his heart. He knew an undivided heart resulted in knowing God, his character and his ways. David recognized that the more intimately he knew God, the more his heart would beat in rhythm with God's heart–guiding him away from deception and toward a life that would honor the name of God. Is it any wonder God described David as "a man after his own heart"?

"You (King Saul) acted foolishly," Samuel said.
"You have not kept the command the Lord your God gave you;
if you had, he would have established your kingdom over Israel for all time.
But now your kingdom will not endure;
the Lord has sought out <u>a man after his own heart (David)</u> and appointed him leader of his people, because you have not kept the Lord's command."
1 Samuel 13:13-14 (emphasis mine)

* * * * *

Young Isaac was still uncertain. "Father, you said you have knowledge in the ways of the serpent, yet you speak of the 'fear of the Lord' as being the source of true knowledge. I am confused. Should I study the ways of the serpent or the ways of the Lord?"

Leaning against his staff, Abraham struck a thoughtful pose. "Oh, Isaac, you have many questions. I wonder if Jehovah will give me length of days to answer them all. Your question is a wise one and my answer is this: 'Above all else, study the teachings of Jehovah.' Hide them in your heart, my son. For it will be knowledge of the Holy One that will reveal to you when the serpent is near. Such knowledge will distance you from his deceptive venom and lead you to safety."

I have hidden your word in my heart
that I might not sin against you.
Psalm 119:11

Do Not Bear False Witness

PRINCIPLES

1. Our desires can deceive us.
2. Satan will add to God's word in order to deceive us.
3. Sin in our lives makes us want to hide from God.
4. Rather than assume personal responsibility for our sin, our nature is to blame others.
5. Blaming others for our sin is a hindrance to true repentance.
6. True repentance involves more than feeling sorry for the consequences of our sin.
7. True repentance results in changed behavior.
8. Our sin is not as big as God's mercy.
9. It is God's nature to be merciful.
10. As Christians, we should want lips that are free from any trace of deception.
11. A baby snake is still a snake; a baby lie is still a lie.
12. Baby snakes grow.
13. The fear of the Lord is the beginning of wisdom.
14. A hypocrite deceives himself and others by pretending to be something he is not.
15. God's duty to judge does not negate his ability to love.
16. God's love endures beyond his judgment.

Do Not Bear False Witness

DISCUSSION QUESTIONS

1. How would you describe Adam's and Eve's confessions of their sin?

2. Why is the description of Satan as an "angel of light" particularly accurate? (2 Corinthians 11:14)

3. What is the root of our temptations? (James 1:14)

4. Why does a divided heart make us unstable?

5. Who or what are you blaming for a present sin in your life?

6. Can you identify a lie you've believed that has stunted your spiritual growth?

7. How do you feel when your child sins and then tries to hide from you?

8. How does being a hypocrite relate to bearing false witness?

9. Can you identify a mask you may be wearing?

May I never boast except in the cross of our Lord Jesus Christ,
through which the world has been crucified to me, and I to the world.

Galatians 6:14

Chapter 10

Do Not Covet

Exodus 20:17

"Food, Flattery, and Finances"

In this chapter you will learn about:

- aspects of the world we're tempted to covet;
- the meaning of "temperance" as it relates to coveting;
- the consequences of coveting food and drink;
- characteristics of the prideful person;
- why God gives wealth to a person.

Hebrew/Greek word studies: covet, flesh, pride, eyes, cheerful

When we got our tithing statement from our church, our son's statement was on a separate sheet of paper from ours. We told Aaron his giving that year had been $6.00. "But I know I've given a lot more money than that." His daddy told him they only keep a record of the money he puts in the church envelope but not any loose money given. "Oh, I don't care what they say. God is keeping the real record and he knows it all."
Aaron Menser, Feb. 3, 1986, age 8

To covet something is to delight in, to desire or to lust after something or someone.

Do not love the world or the things in the world.
If anyone loves the world, the love of the Father is not in him.
For all that is in the world–the lust of the <u>*flesh*</u>*, the lust of the* <u>*eyes*</u>*, and the* <u>*pride*</u> *of life–*
is not of the Father but is of the world. And the world is passing away, and the lust of it;
but he who does the will of God abides forever.
1 John 2:15-17 (NKJV) (emphases mine)

Our *flesh* is our physical body, as opposed to our soul or spirit. The flesh encompasses our human nature with its frailties, both physical and moral. To lust with our *eyes* entails the idea of being envious, as from a jealous side-glance. Being *prideful,* or boastful about what a person has or does, means to put confidence in "self" rather than in God.

We'll learn that the desire to covet is defeated when we rely on God to meet our needs. Finally, we'll learn that blessings and wealth are given so we can be generous to those in need, which ultimately brings glory to God.

You will be made rich in every way so that you can be generous on every occasion,
and through us your generosity will result in thanksgiving to God.
2 Corinthians 9:11

The way it might have been. . .

"Speak one at a time," said Isaac.

"But it was Grandfather Abraham who went to Sodom," insisted Jacob.

"You're wrong. It was Lot, the nephew of our grandfather who went to that wicked city," insisted Esau.

Isaac spoke softly, "Please, sons, no more strife. It's true Lot chose to live in Sodom, but it was my father, your grandfather Abraham, whose prayers lifted Lot out of that burning city. I see there is need to tell the story again. You must understand it well, for the generations to follow will need to know its meaning."

GREEDY WEALTH

Lot looked up and saw that the whole plain of the Jordan was well watered,
like the garden of the Lord, like the land of Egypt, toward Zoar.
(This was before the Lord destroyed Sodom and Gomorrah.)
So Lot chose for himself the whole plain of the Jordan and set out toward the east.
The two men parted company: Abram lived in the land of Canaan,
while Lot lived among the cities of the plain and pitched his tents near Sodom.
Then the Lord said, "The outcry against Sodom and Gomorrah
is so great and their sin so grievous that I will go down and see if
what they have done is as bad as the outcry that has reached me. If not, I will know."
Genesis 13:10–12, Genesis 18:20–21

Grievous sins, exceedingly wicked sins—this is where Lot took his family and his wealth, to a city renowned for immorality. Eventually, however, this "well-watered" plain of Jordan, saturated with all manner of perversion, would be charred with the judgment of God Almighty.

Were Lot's motives for settling near Sodom self-serving? Was greed his reason for choosing the prime grazing land for his herds and flocks? Was Lot himself drawn to the sensual environment of Sodom? Rather than make a quick judgment about Lot, let's slow down and see what we can learn from him.

Ultimately, we'll find the once wealthy and prosperous Lot living in a cave. Sodom is in ashes; the vegetation of the land has been wiped out and the same fire that destroyed Sodom has consumed all of Lot's wealth. Lot's wife is dead and, while under the influence of wine, Lot impregnates both of his daughters, resulting in children who will eventually become bitter enemies of Israel (Genesis 19:36–38). Suddenly, a deafening silence is heard across the mountains of Zoar.

But Lot didn't plan to fail; no one ever does. Lot merely "saw" the fertile plains of the Jordan. It didn't take long for Lot to enter the city of Sodom—and once inside its border, he felt an overwhelming force.

You shall not covet your neighbor's house.
You shall not covet your neighbor's wife, or his manservant or maidservant,
his ox or donkey, or anything that belongs to your neighbor.
Exodus 20:17

Covet: Hebrew, *chamad* (khaw-mad´): to delight in, to desire, to lust after

To help understand why Lot was drawn to a city like Sodom, let's be reminded that God formed man from the *dust of the ground* (Genesis 2:7a). God used dirt, humus, *the world* to form man's physical body. We're human and our flesh has an inherent attraction to the things of the world.

Coveting can begin innocently, with a look, a glance, perhaps a second glance. But beware: for coveting has the ability to grow into a craving force. Soon this desire consumes our thoughts and energies. Pangs of envy are upon us, and whether it's that second piece of pie, another drink, a new wardrobe, a new car, a larger home, more land, or even the "well-watered plain of the Jordan," we're not content until our craving is fed and (temporarily) satisfied.

LUST OF THE FLESH

Do not love the world or the things in the world.
If anyone loves the world, the love of the Father is not in him.
For all that is in the world–
the lust of the flesh, the lust of the eyes, and the pride of life–
is not of the Father but is of the world.
1 John 2:15–16 (NKJV)

Flesh: Greek, *sarx* (sarx): the body as opposed to the soul; our human nature with its frailties, both physical and moral

Our flesh includes all of our physical appetites. To "lust after the flesh" is to have an uncontrolled desire, appetite, or passion.

Following the baptism of Jesus in the Jordan river, Jesus' flesh was put to the test:

Jesus was led by the Spirit into the desert to be tempted by the devil.
After fasting forty days and forty nights, he was hungry.
The tempter came to him and said,
"If you are the Son of God, tell these stones to become bread."
Matthew 4:1–3 (emphasis mine)

"Jesus, I know you're hungry. Fill that empty belly—that is, *if* you're the Son of God."

Do you not know that your body is a temple of the Holy Spirit,
who is in you, whom you have received from God?
You are not your own; you were bought at a price.
Therefore honor God with your body.
Therefore, I urge you, brothers, in view of God's mercy, to offer your bodies as living sacrifices, holy and pleasing to God–this is your spiritual act of worship.
1 Corinthians 6:19–20, Romans 12:1

Our bodies are a reflection of Christ living in us. It's sad to say, but many Christian "homes" don't accurately reflect its Occupant. The truth is: our bodies speak for themselves as to our relationship with food and drink. Without speaking a word, a body can say, "Food is my god. I love, adore, covet and even worship it." (Have I mentioned I'm not liking writing this chapter?) On the other hand, there are bodies that say to the world: "I believe Christ lives in me and gives me strength to say 'no' to the cravings of my flesh. I want my body, as much as is within my power, to reflect the Holy Spirit living inside of me."

It's an eternal, one-time act of commitment to trust God with our spirits, but to give God control of our bodies is a *daily* choice. Our flesh is prone to crave the pleasures of the world. But cravings are rarely silenced; they're impatient and demand immediate gratification. And if cravings aren't given their way, irritability soon sets in. What can we expect to happen when we routinely feed the cravings of our flesh?

Listen, my son, and be wise, and keep your heart on the right path.
Do not join those who drink too much wine or gorge themselves on meat,
for drunkards and gluttons become poor, and drowsiness clothes them in rags.
Proverbs 23:19–21 (emphases mine)

Being poor and feeling drowsy is a lousy way to live. Resources are diminished, resulting in less productivity, which in turn results in even fewer resources. It's a slippery slope that reminds me very much of a seductive serpent.

The sayings of King Lemuel–an oracle his mother taught him:
"O my son, O son of my womb, O son of my vows,
do not spend your strength on women, your vigor on those who ruin kings.
It is not for kings, O Lemuel–not for kings to drink wine,
not for rulers to crave beer,
lest they drink and forget what the law decrees,
and deprive all the oppressed of their rights.
Proverbs 31:1-5 (emphasis mine)

There it is, the reason we're not to give in to the desires of our flesh: overindulgence causes us to *forget what the law decrees.* Sleepy and stumbling, now we've wandered outside of God's boundaries, where all kinds of bad things can happen to us.

Even when the flesh has its way and thinks it has won, actually it has lost. Think for a moment of the person who serves his flesh and the rewards he receives. Many "winners" carry the trophies of high blood pressure and cholesterol levels, heart disease, obesity, diabetes, alcoholism, lung disease, sexually transmitted diseases . . .

Has the lust of the flesh gained a foothold in your life? Have you looked to the world to satisfy your hungry spirit? If so, please take comfort in the following words:

As a father has compassion on his children,
so the Lord has compassion on those who fear him;
for he knows how we are formed,
he remembers that we are dust.
Psalm 103:13–14

God knows our attraction to the world is normal. He remembers kneeling to the ground, lifting the rich, moist dirt into his hands and creating man in his own image. He knows where we came from. But he also knows we are far more than a human body, more than flesh and bones; for within our body lives the spirit-man also created by God. This spirit-man has his desires as well, the main one being the need for fellowship with his Father.

Daily we choose the food that will nourish our bodies, but are we as deliberate in feeding our spirits? How often do we go to the table of God's fellowship and partake of his heavenly food? Dear friend, God has prepared a table for us, and he is always ready to receive guests.

TEMPERANCE

Then I realized that it is good and proper for a man to eat and drink,
and to find satisfaction in his toilsome labor under the sun
during the few days of life God has given him–for this is his lot.
Moreover, when God gives any man wealth and possessions,
and enables him to enjoy them, to accept his lot
and be happy in his work–this is a gift of God.
Ecclesiastes 5:18–19

When creating mankind, God could have formed us any way he chose. God chose to create us with the ability to enjoy life, food, our work, our wealth, and sexual relations with our spouses. God wants us to smile and find pleasure in the things our flesh was made to enjoy. Contrary to what many believe, God is generous toward his children, withholding no good thing from those he loves. God's only stipulation is that his goodness be enjoyed within the boundaries of his commandments.

Our culture generally relates the word "lust" to the area of sexuality. But did you know it's possible to lust after food and drink? Yes, God created man with the physical need for food and drink, and he wants us to enjoy both; but just as God blesses our sexuality within the covenant of marriage, God blesses our consumption of food and drink within the confines of temperance.

Temperance denotes a lifestyle of moderation. The temperate man is self-restrained, with the emphasis on *self*. No one forces the temperate man to eat and drink in a controlled fashion. Rather, it's his personal choice to avoid excessive behavior.

"Everything is permissible for me"–but not everything is beneficial.
"Everything is permissible for me"–but I will not be mastered by anything.
"Food for stomach and the stomach for food"–but God will destroy them both.
The body is not meant for sexual immorality, but for the Lord,
and the Lord for the body.
1 Corinthians 6:12–13

We should be careful not to understate the discipline and determination it takes for our spirit to have victory over our flesh. *It is a battle*. The apostle Paul likened this battle to a boxing match.

Everyone who competes in the games goes into strict training.
They do it to get a crown that will not last;
but we do it to get a crown that will last forever.
Therefore I do not run like a man running aimlessly;
I do not fight like a man beating the air.
No, I beat my body and make it my slave so that after I have preached to others,
I myself will not be disqualified for the prize.
1 Corinthians 9:25–27

THE PRIDE OF LIFE

Satan soon realized the lust of the flesh had no power over Jesus. Though hungry after forty days without food, Jesus did not turn the stones into bread. Not to be discouraged, if the Son of God couldn't be tempted through his belly, Satan would simply pull out another weapon and aim it at a different place.

Then the devil took him to the holy city
and had him stand on the highest point of the temple.
"If you are the Son of God," he said, "throw yourself down. For it is written:
" 'He will command his angels concerning you, and they will lift you up in their hands,
so that you will not strike your foot against a stone.' "
Matthew 4:5-6

So, you say you're God's son? Then jump from the top of the temple and see if your daddy rescues you. He has angels he can send to protect you–if you're really his son–if he even cares.

Oh, how tempting it must have been for Jesus to defend his heritage. It was, after all, a Godly one. But Jesus took neither pride nor privilege in being the Son of God, for he reasoned that even his heritage was not his own, in that it was given to him by his Father.

Disciplined Christian, beware. Though the lusts of your flesh may be mastered, though your lifestyle is disciplined and healthy, Satan has plans to tempt you through *the pride of your life.* He will even tempt you to be proud that your flesh is disciplined and under the Spirit's control. How cunning is that?

Satan has a tackle box with hooks and bait and lures all designed to tempt you in the area where you're most vulnerable. He'll tempt you to be proud of your education, proud of your heritage, your stock portfolio, your retirement fund, your home, and your children. And if you're not an overtly proud person, he'll tempt you to be proud of your humility.

Do not love the world or the things in the world.
If anyone loves the world, the love of the Father is not in him.
For all that is in the world–
the lust of the flesh, the lust of the eyes, and the pride of life–
is not of the Father but is of the world.
1 John 2:15–16 (NKJV)

Pride: Greek, *alazoneia* (al-ad-zon-i′-a): self confidence; to brag, to boast

In his arrogance the wicked man . . . boasts of the cravings of his heart. . .
In his pride the wicked does not seek him; in all his thoughts there is no room for God.
His ways are always prosperous; he is haughty and your laws are far from him;
he sneers at all his enemies. He says to himself,
"Nothing will shake me; I'll always be happy and never have trouble."
Psalm 10:2–6

Let's say it plain to be heard. The prideful person . . .

- is arrogant;
- boasts about the cravings of his heart;
- does not seek the Lord;
- has no room for God in his heart;
- is always prosperous;
- is haughty;
- keeps God's laws far from him;
- sneers at his enemies;
- thinks nothing will shake him;
- thinks he will always be happy;
- thinks he will never have trouble.

The prideful man desires the praises of men. Sitting on his pinnacle of performance, this individual positions himself so that men must look up to him. He may even go so far as to mock or make sarcastic remarks concerning people whom he considers beneath him. Haughty and arrogant, the prideful man lives in delusion, having an exaggerated opinion of his own importance. Oftentimes it's difficult for the pride-filled to settle for anything less than he thinks a person of his caliber deserves. Pride is a form of idolatry, as it allows man to worship himself. But trouble is promised to the pompous.

Pride goes before destruction, a haughty spirit before a fall.
"For everyone who exalts himself will be humbled,
and he who humbles himself will be exalted."
Proverbs 16:18, Luke 18:14b

I'm the Son of God. I was born from a virgin. I endured forty days in the desert without water or food. I've healed leprosy, a shriveled hand, and a woman sick from bleeding. I've walked on water and raised the dead. . .

All this, yet Jesus described himself as a gentle and humble man.

"Come to me, all you who are weary and burdened, and I will give you rest.
Take my yoke upon you and learn from me, for I am gentle and humble in heart,
and you will find rest for your souls."
Matthew 11:28–29 (emphases mine)

THE LUST OF THE EYES

For all that is in the world–
the lust of the flesh and the lust of the eyes, and the pride of life–
is not of the Father but is of the world.
1 John 2:16

Eyes: Greek, *ophthalmos* (of-thal-mos'): figuratively speaking, it means envy, as from a jealous side-glance

Again, the devil took him to a very high mountain
and showed him all the kingdoms of the world and their splendor.
"All this I will give you," he said, "if you will bow down and worship me."
Jesus said to him, "Away from me, Satan.
For it is written: 'Worship the Lord your God, and serve him only.' "
Matthew 4:8–10 (emphasis mine)

At this time in history, Satan was the prince of the world (John 14:30), and the world was his to offer to Jesus, "If you will bow down and worship me." But Jesus won't prematurely take what's eternally his. There has to be the shedding of blood—the cross is before him.

"I (Jesus) will not speak with you much longer,
for the prince of this world is coming.
He has no hold on me, but the world must learn that
I love the Father and that I do exactly what my Father has commanded me."
John 14:31 (addition mine)

HOW DRY ARE YOUR EYES?

Years ago I was diagnosed with dry-eye disease. In essence, my tear glands don't produce enough tears and my meibomian glands don't produce proper eye lubrication. (Did you even know you have meibomian glands?) And so my eyes are very dry and irritated. Now that's an understatement if I ever wrote one. There are days when my eyes hurt so badly I'm housebound, under humidifiers, and in excruciating pain. I finally had to have tiny plugs put in my tear ducts to hold on to what tears I do produce. No, that wasn't enough relief. Next, my tear ducts were literally cauterized to permanently close them so that what tears I do produce won't drain down my nose. My eyes need every precious drop. Part of the treatment for dry-eye disease have been drops that sting, ointments that blur my vision, and care to avoid the wind.

Hopefully you won't ever have to go through the dry-eye scenario. But surely you've had times when shampoo stung your eyes, a contact lens has been off-center, or a piece of sand or an eyelash got stuck in your eye. Can you remember the agitation it produced? "My eyes, my eyes! I'm in pain! Do something, quick!"

When your eyes hurt, that's all you can think about. The pain is tormenting. It makes you feel nervous and on edge. *I think that's what happens to eyes that covet.* Our eyes become red and inflamed with envy, as we see others possessing the things we think should be ours. It's all we can think about. Once our vision is blurred, we tend to panic and become confused. We may stumble a bit, lose our way for a while and make decisions and purchases we wouldn't normally make. We are, after all, watery-eyed and pitiful.

As my dry-eye disease progressed, I found myself in further distress. As a long-term result of irritated and inflamed eyes, calloused "threads" had developed inside my left eye. Imagine, if you will, how calluses form on your fingers when learning to play the guitar. First your fingers are red and sore, then they become blistered, and eventually calluses form. Talk about painful. I told my ophthalmologist, "I can hardly make it though the day. Even with my eyes closed I'm still in pain."

I think we could relate this same progression of callousness to coveting the things of the world. The constant irritation of continually wanting more and more causes us to become calloused to the blessings God has already given to us. Without realizing it, a continual lifestyle of ingratitude and coveting can result in some very hard and painful consequences.

The flip side to coveting is being grateful for God's blessings in our lives. This kind of gratitude makes us thankful for the provisions God has given us and encourages us to be confident that he will provide for our future needs as well. We put our desires in the hand of God and trust him to lead us toward what's best for our lives.

That's the kind of faith Abraham possessed. While Lot "chose for himself" the well-watered plain of Jordan, a land that would ultimately be burned and destroyed, Abraham had made the decision, years earlier, to allow God to choose where he would live.

By faith Abraham,
when called to go to a place he would later receive as his inheritance,
obeyed and went, even though he did not know where he was going.
By faith he made his home in the promised land like a stranger in a foreign country;
he lived in tents, as did Isaac and Jacob, who were heirs with him of the same promise.
For he was looking forward to the city with foundations,
whose architect and builder is God.
Hebrews 11:8–10

Abraham was farsighted. By faith he was able to look forward to the future God had promised him. Covetous eyes are nearsighted. Not only are they red with envy, they have a short-term-got-to-have-it-right-now-attitude.

Nearsighted eyes can't see into the distance, specifically, the eternal distance. They only see what's right in front of them, and they make decisions based on what will bring them immediate pleasure, oftentimes disregarding the long-term consequences of their choices. Again, covetous eyes may not see clearly, but they *speak* very clearly, telling us they'll quit itching and stinging as soon as we acquire their desire.

FEARFUL OR CHEERFUL

By now we've surely learned that God is all about faith. Faith in God is a big deal to God. Having faith means we know God, his character, and his promise to provide. Fear is the opposite of faith. Fear tells us to gather extra manna and stockpile God's blessings, just in case he decides to leave us hungry. Deep down, we . . .

Feel
Everything is
A
Responsibility

Fear tells us we must take total responsibility for ourselves. Being fearful is an indicator that we don't know God well enough to trust him to provide for our needs. So, we'll do it ourselves, thank you very much. As I write these words I remember hearing my toddlers say, "I do it myself." That attitude was good and proper for two-year-olds, as they're learning new skills and growing toward maturity, but it reeks of spiritual immaturity coming from an adult. God doesn't want us to "do it ourselves." He wants us to depend on him and have faith in his care for us. That doesn't mean we sit on the couch and do nothing; it means we give it our best effort, realizing it's God who gives us the strength to even get up from that couch and be able to go to work. Then, we trust God with the outcome of our efforts and *give him the glory* for giving us the ability to work and produce wealth. If we fail to recognize this and think we've "done it ourselves," we'll take pride in and credit for what our efforts have produced.

You may say to yourself,
"My power and the strength of my hands have produced this wealth for me."
But remember the Lord your God,
for it is he who gives you the ability to produce wealth,
and so confirms his covenant, which he swore to your forefathers, as it is today.
Deuteronomy 8:17–18

Deep down, the greedy person is a needy person, fearfully uneasy about his future and continually on guard against an unexpected (or should I say "expected") misfortune. The greedy lack faith in the goodness of God.

And everything that does not come from faith is sin.
Romans 14:23b

Now let's see what faith-filled generosity looks like:

Each man should give what he has decided in his heart to give,
not reluctantly or under compulsion,
for God loves a cheerful giver.
2 Corinthians 9:7

Cheerful: Greek, *hilaros* (hil-ar-os'): merry to the point of hilarious

Is there a grimace on our faces when we give to the Lord, or are we smiling so big we can barely hold back a laugh? Do we look forward to scattering our wealth? Do we *enjoy* the act of giving?

You will be made rich in every way
so that you can be generous on every occasion,
and through us your generosity will result in thanksgiving to God.
2 Corinthians 9:11

It's not a sin to be wealthy. God makes us rich so we can be generous to others, resulting in others being thankful to God and, in their–and our–gratitude, God is glorified. We should always see any generosity which comes our way as coming from God, through the hands of others, to us.

Jesus was a giver. He never hoarded the riches of the world *he* created. Though Jesus enjoyed the natural pleasures of food and drink, no one ever looked at Jesus and saw evidence of gluttony or drunkenness. His holy eyes never experienced the act of coveting. His dress was that of a servant. If Jesus ever looked into a mirror, he saw the reflection of meekness and humility. Self could not be found, for the Son of God relinquished any rights to self in order to claim total dependence upon his Father.

We're made from the world. Our flesh will crave the things of the world. But if we're believers in Christ, we can look at our flesh from the perspective of the cross. As believers, our flesh is dead. *Our flesh* was crucified *with Christ.*

I have been crucified with Christ and I no longer live,
but Christ lives in me.
The life I live in the body, I live by faith in the Son of God,
who loved me and gave himself for me.
May I never boast except in the cross of our Lord Jesus Christ,
through which the world has been crucified to me, and I to the world.
Galatians 6:14, Galatians 2:20

If you've yet to give your life to Jesus, then you know all too well how alive your flesh can behave. But even as a believer, our positionally and spiritually "dead flesh" still wants control of our bodies. Paul likened this struggle to a boxing match (1 Corinthians 9:27).

After studying what it means to covet, which part of the world keeps raising its ugly head at you? I've circled mine:

- lust of the flesh (fleshly appetites, food, drink, sexual behavior)
- lust of the eyes (power, success, money, materialism)
- pride of life (lack of humility, boastful of accomplishments)

Though tempted by Satan to "bow down and worship me," Jesus' response was, "Get behind me, Satan" (Matthew 4:10). Jesus coveted nothing the world offered him. He didn't bow to his physical appetites, take pride in his godly heritage, or pursue the pleasures of his eyes. Jesus lived a life of daily crucifixion, preparing his flesh for the day it would be asked to hang from a cross.

I am
poured out
like water,
and all my
bones are
out of joint.
My heart has turned to wax; it has melted away within me. My strength is dried
up like a potsherd, and my tongue sticks to the roof of my mouth; you lay me in the
dust of death.
Dogs have
surrounded
me; a band
of evil men
has encircled
me, they have
pierced my
hands and
my feet. I
can count
all my bones;
people stare
and gloat
over me.
Psalm 22:14–17

Do Not Covet

PRINCIPLES

1. God used dirt to form our physical bodies.
2. Our flesh has an inherent attraction to the things of the world.
3. The Lord has compassion on us. He remembers he made us from dust.
4. Cravings are never satisfied, only temporarily calmed.
5. Wealth can go up in smoke.
6. It's a one-time commitment to trust God with our spirits; it is a daily choice to give God control of our flesh.
7. Jesus gave his flesh to purchase our flesh.
8. Pride is a form of self-adoration, as it allows man to worship himself.
9. The prideful person desires the praise of others.
10. The prideful person has an exaggerated opinion of his own importance.
11. Jesus did not walk in pride, and neither should we.
12. Covetous eyes are nearsighted.
13. Faith-filled eyes are farsighted.
14. Coveting is synonymous with greed and idolatry.
15. Everything that does not come from faith is sin.
16. God gives us wealth so we can be generous to others.
17. God loves a cheerful giver.

Do Not Covet

DISCUSSION QUESTIONS

1. What price did God pay for your body? (1 Corinthians 6:20)
2. In what ways can over-eating make a person "poor"?
3. How can over-eating affect the lives of our children?
4. What are some of the consequences of over-drinking?
5. Why are gluttony and drunkenness often used in connection with one another?
6. How does overindulging our flesh affect our thinking skills?
7. Why would a person want to be drowsy rather than active?
8. Can you identify a careless decision you've made while being "drowsy"?
9. Why is our first impulse, oftentimes, to satisfy our flesh rather than our spirit?
10. How can remembering our flesh is never satisfied help us lead temperate lives?
11. What are some accomplishments in your life of which you could be proud?
12. How can you develop meekness in these areas?
13. When you think of a humble person, who comes to mind?
14. When you think of a generous person, who comes to mind?

The commandments,
"Do not commit adultery," "Do not murder,"
"Do not steal," "Do not covet,"
and whatever other commandment there may be,
are summed up in this one rule:
"Love your neighbor as yourself."
And this is love,
that we walk in obedience to his commandments.

Romans 13:9, 2 John 1:6a

Chapter 11

Love One Another

"It's Good for Your Heart"

In this chapter you will learn:

- the purpose of the Ten Commandments before salvation;
- the purpose of the Ten Commandments after salvation;
- Jesus' role in fulfilling the Old Testament Law;
- what it means to "believe in Jesus Christ";
- benefits of delighting in God's laws.

Hebrew/Greek word studies: rubbish, fulfill, burdensome, grace, new, greatest, examine, saved, justified

Once we accept Christ into our hearts, a miracle takes place. The finger of God that once wrote the Ten Commandments on tablets of stone now writes these same laws somewhere else.

"This is the covenant I will make with them after that time, says the Lord, I will put my laws in their hearts, and I will write them on their minds."
Hebrews 10:16

At salvation, the Person of the Holy Spirit comes to live within us, changing our hearts into hearts that enjoy pleasing God. God's desires become our desires, his delight our delight, his commandments our commandments. And because God is love, he will express himself through acts of love.

The entire law is summed up in a single command:
"Love your neighbor as yourself."
Galatians 5:14

> It's August 1987. After taking his bath, John Michael scampers downstairs where his daddy decides to check out Little John's bathing skills. Four-year-old John dutifully raises both arms for inspection. That's when Mike notices the sweaty signs of a hot summer day sticking to his little boy's armpits. "Son, you need to go back to the tub and do a better job of washing yourself. You're still dirty." "But Daddy, " John replies, "I *nebber* wash under *there*!"

Adam and Eve failed God miserably when they ate from the tree of the knowledge of good and evil. Then, rather than assume responsibility for their sin, they blamed each other, God, and the serpent for their behavior.

Then the man said, "The woman whom You gave to be with me,
she gave me of the tree and I ate."
And the Lord God said to the woman, "What is this you have done?"
The woman said, "The serpent deceived me, and I ate."
Genesis 3:12–13

Abraham was called a "friend of God." His devotion to God was tested when God asked Abraham to sacrifice his son, Isaac, to the Lord. Abraham passed that all-important test, but not before he'd failed an earlier one.

Now there was a famine in the land,
and Abram went down to Egypt to live there for a while because the famine was severe.
As he was about to enter Egypt, he said to his wife Sarai,
"I know what a beautiful woman you are. When the Egyptians see you, they will say,
'This is his wife.' Then they will kill me but will let you live.
Say you are my sister, so that I will be treated well for your sake
and my life will be spared because of you."
Genesis 12:10–13

Fear persuaded Abraham to lie about his relationship with Sarai. Abraham, a man of great faith and remembered as a friend of God, was a spiritual giant who fell into fear. Afraid the Egyptians would kill him if they knew Sarah was his wife, Abraham bore false witness and asked Sarah to do the same.

And Sarah, when God told her she would bear a son in her old age, laughed at his words. Forgetful of the God of the Sabbath, the One who provides for our needs and with whom nothing is impossible, Sarah not only laughed at God's word, but then lied to him.

Then the Lord said,
"I will surely return to you about this time next year,
and Sarah your wife will have a son."
Now Sarah was listening at the entrance to the tent, which was behind him.
Abraham and Sarah were already old and well advanced in years,
and Sarah was past the age of childbearing.
So Sarah laughed to herself as she thought,
"After I am worn out and my master is old, will I now have this pleasure?"
Then the Lord said to Abraham, "Why did Sarah laugh and say,
'Will I really have a child, now that I am old?' Is anything too hard for the Lord?
I will return to you at the appointed time next year and Sarah will have a son."
Sarah was afraid, so she lied and said, "I did not laugh."
But he said, "Yes, you did laugh."
Genesis 18:10–15 (emphasis mine)

Isaac, the son Sarah laughed about and doubted would ever be born, followed almost exactly in his father's fearful footsteps.

When the men of that place asked him about his wife,
he (Isaac) said, "She is my sister," because he was afraid to say, "She is my wife."
He thought, "The men of this place might kill me on account of Rebekah,
because she is beautiful."
Genesis 26:7 (emphasis mine)

Isaac's wife, Rebekah, was a woman of many virtues. She was a beautiful virgin, a willing worker, generous and hospitable (Genesis 24:16, 25). But Rebekah had her weaknesses. Scripture reveals a major character flaw in Rebekah when she failed to trust God with the future of her favored son, Jacob. Fear led Rebekah to eavesdrop, scheme, and even bear false witness to her husband (Genesis 27:5–10).

In an almost predictable fashion, the children of Isaac and Rebekah struggled with the same sins their parents did. Their son, Jacob, was renowned for his disposition to deceive, and Esau, due to the injustices in his life, for a time carried within him the heart of a murderer.

We all have weak areas in our lives, generational strongholds we struggle with and that must be addressed. Is yours breaking the Sabbath by worrying and forgetting that God has already provided for your needs? Perhaps you make every effort to control the lusts of your flesh, only to find yourself dry-eyed and coveting the things of the world. Maybe fear is your weakness, and you need faith to take off your mask, stop bearing false witness and be your authentic self. Like Little John, you may need to look places you *nebber* wash to find the sin that, after all these years, is still sticking to your life.

All together now, let's raise up our dirty little armpits! Oh my, I see more than one commandment not being lived out in my life. What do you see hiding under there?

1. Have no other gods before God.
2. Do not make an idol in the form of anything.
3. Do not take the Lord's name in vain.
4. Remember the Sabbath.
5. Honor your parents.
6. Do not murder.
7. Do not commit adultery.
8. Do not steal.
9. Do not bear false witness.
10. Do not covet.

The patriarchs of our faith were the cream of the Judeo-Christian crop, yet many times they failed miserably. Let's learn from them. Let's ask ourselves a very tough question: "Where am I vulnerable?" This question may be hard to answer because, like the Hebrews who once lived in Egyptian bondage, our mindset may still be one of bondage rather than of freedom, of fear rather than of faith. What lie have you believed? You know, the one that produces fear and causes you to doubt God's word.

The lie that says, "You're weak and wounded. I can take away your pain if you'll bow down and worship me." That one.

Please feel free to take this prayer as your own:

> *Dear Lord, first I want to thank you for your patience with me throughout the years. I've turned away from you with my sin when I should have trusted your love for me. I'm ready to walk in truth. Please shine light on the lies I've believed and the defeat they've produced in my life. I want to be free of the lies that shackle me to my past. Amen.*

JUSTIFIED

In the last few months I've had to purchase a 7X magnifying mirror to be able to see to put on makeup, pluck eyebrows and do all those other fun things we women do to keep up appearances. I thank God for magnification, for without it I would be walking around thinking I was looking just fine, not even realizing the shape my face was really in. That's what the Ten Commandments did for us. When the law was added, our sin was magnified so that we could see how dirty we really were and *how desperately we need a Savior to clean us up.*

What shall we say, then? Is the law sin? Certainly not!
Indeed I would not have known what sin was except through the law.
For I would not have known what coveting really was if the law had not said, "Do not covet."
But sin, seizing the opportunity afforded by the commandment, produced in me every kind of covetous desire.
For apart from law, sin is dead.
Romans 7:7–8 (emphasis mine)

Knowing what sin is actually stimulates our interest in sin. And it's the law that initially defines sin for us. But here comes the beauty of seeing our sin.

The law was added so that the trespass might increase.
But where sin increased, grace increased all the more . . .
Romans 5:20 (emphasis mine)

The law was added for two distinct purposes:

1. so that our trespass might increase (become larger, be magnified); and
2. so that grace could increase all the more.

On our own, we're simply not capable of keeping God's commandments. Our flesh is too weak to obey or, perhaps better stated, too strong to surrender.

For what the law could not do in that it was weak through the flesh, God did by sending His own Son in the likeness of sinful flesh, on account of sin: He condemned sin in the flesh, that the righteous requirement of the law might be fulfilled in us who do not walk according to the flesh but according to the Spirit.
Romans 8:3–4 (NKJV; emphasis mine)

God did it himself. God fulfilled the requirements of his law by *providing himself* to die on our behalf. He did this so that we would be made righteous and worthy of a relationship with him. He wants us back in the Garden with him.

So the law was put in charge to lead us to Christ that we might be justified by faith.
Galatians 3:24

Justified: Greek, *dikaioo* (dik-ah-yo'-o): to render just or innocent, to be righteous, to be made holy

BUILT UPON GRACE

After the death and resurrection of Jesus there arose a man who was "full of God's grace and power" (Acts 6:8a). "Grace" and "power" were unfamiliar phenomena to the religious leaders of that day, so much so that their very presence was perceived as a threat. So intimidating was the power of God in this man's life that the members of the local synagogue tried to argue against the validity of his testimony, "but they could not stand up against his wisdom or the Spirit by whom he spoke" (Acts 6:10).

The man was Stephen. And when Stephen dared to imply that God did not live in their temple, they accused Stephen of speaking against the holy place.

"However, the Most High does not dwell in temples made with hands, as the prophet says: 'Heaven is My throne, and the earth is My footstool. What house will you build for Me?' " says the Lord.
Acts 7:48–49a (NKJV)

God asks us the same question, "What house will you build for Me?" Whether we realize it or not, we're answering his question. Even giving no answer is an answer. Our culture lends itself to accepting the opinions of the world and the traditions of men as the cornerstone for our homes. This is one answer to God's question. But there's a far better one, that of laying a foundation for our homes that isn't based on our culture but on our Christ.

Perhaps you have regrets concerning the way you've built your home. You may feel distanced from God because of these choices, and now you're attempting to earn back God's favor. You're willing to work hard, sweat profusely, do whatever it takes to reinforce your shaky family structure. Please don't work so hard. Try to keep in mind that God doesn't expect us to build houses by our own strength. That's too big of a job for us. The very purpose of the New Covenant is to allow the Holy Spirit to come and live inside us, changing each heart from one of self-effort and fatigue to a heart that's God-focused and empowered. The Holy Spirit is the power source of our new hearts. We can rest in the good news that, when we have Christ living in us, he provides *his* strength for any task that lies ahead.

Unless the Lord builds the house, its builders labor in vain.
Psalm 127:1a

In Acts, Chapter 7, Stephen gave quite a discourse on the heritage upon which Abraham, Isaac, and Jacob built their homes. Stephen tells how Joseph's and Moses' lives were built upon the bedrock of faith in God and his promises. Stephen challenged the religious leaders to build their lives not on the works of their flesh but on the finished work of Christ and the

Person of the Holy Spirit. And, as if speaking about Jesus and the Holy Spirit weren't enough to incur the wrath of these leaders, Stephen ended his speech talking about angels, the persecution of prophets, and the murder of the Righteous Son of God (Acts 7:51–52). The purpose of Stephen's speech was to offer these leaders freedom from themselves and their efforts to secure eternal life.

But these leaders had become "capable caterpillars," carrying the weight of the law quite efficiently upon their broad, proud shoulders. In their minds they'd sacrificed and suffered, and endured to varying degrees the demands of God's laws and, as a result of their burdensome lifestyles, they'd earned a measure of much enjoyed respect in their church and communities. Now a nobody-named-Stephen was asking them to trade in their hard-earned reputations for a freely given relationship with God. Build our lives upon *grace*—blasphemy!

When they heard this, they were furious and gnashed their teeth at him. But Stephen, full of the Holy Spirit, looked up to heaven and saw the glory of God, and Jesus standing at the right hand of God. "Look," he said, "I see heaven open and the Son of Man standing at the right hand of God." At this they covered their ears and, yelling at the top of their voices, they all rushed at him, dragged him out of the city and began to stone him.
Meanwhile, the witnesses laid their clothes at the feet of a young man named Saul.
Acts 7:54–58

When the truth of God's word revealed the futility of their works, the Sanhedrin's pride was deeply wounded. Exposed, the Sanhedrin became so furious with Stephen that they literally "gnashed their teeth at him" (Acts 7:54b). How dare Stephen suggest they were stiff-necked? And the ultimate insult was to accuse them of being uncircumcised, the modern-day equivalent of not belonging to the family of God.

THE METAMORPHOSIS OF SAUL

> Eating at Burger King after church, talking with my younger son, John: "Son, what was your Sunday School lesson about today?" Between bites of cheeseburger and fries: "It was about that man who denied Jesus three times while Jesus was being *crossified.*" ~ John Menser, age 9

As a young man, Saul heartily approved of the stoning and death of Stephen. One day, however, as Saul traveled the dusty road to Damascus with intentions of persecuting even more believers in Christ, Saul's opinion of Stephen changed. Yes, Saul was physically circumcised (signifying his Jewish heritage), but his heart wasn't exposed to the grace of God (Acts 7:51). Stephen was right: Saul's *heart* was not circumcised.

Then, the day came when Saul (later called Paul), a man guilty of refusing Jesus, rejecting the Holy Spirit, and an accomplice to murder, fell hard to the ground and heard a voice saying to him:

"Saul, Saul, why do you persecute me?"
Acts 9:4

Trembling and astonished, blinded for three days by the light of God's truth, Saul was led by friends to the home of a man named Judas. There Paul's sight was restored and he was filled with the Holy Spirit and baptized (Acts 9:17–18).

Saul thought he'd done a good—no, a faultless job of serving God. He'd been educated in the finest religious school of the day, trained by the respected teacher Gamaliel (Acts 5:34, 22:3), and was an expert in the law of Moses. Why, he'd even given consent to the stoning of the heretic, Stephen, a man who dared suggest that attempting to keep God's laws would not secure eternal life. Without question, Saul was a dedicated follower of God, disciplined in his daily routine and dependable in his religious activities.

If anyone else thinks he has reasons to put confidence in the flesh, I have more:

circumcised on the eighth day, of the people of Israel, of the tribe of Benjamin,
a Hebrew of Hebrews; in regard to the law, a Pharisee;
as for zeal, persecuting the church; as for legalistic righteousness, faultless.
Philippians 3:4b–6

Credentials. These were Saul's. But even with his education, lineage, religious activities and legalistic perfection, something was lacking. He was without power. He didn't know grace and was a stranger to the Holy Spirit. Saul, a man who'd arguably lived the closest thing to a perfect life as is humanly possible, was overwhelmed when his "lawful life" was compared to a life based on knowing Christ and experiencing his mercy.

But whatever was to my profit
I now consider loss for the sake of Christ.
What is more, I consider everything a loss
compared to the surpassing greatness of knowing Christ Jesus my Lord,
for whose sake I have lost all things. I consider them rubbish,
that I may gain Christ and be found in him,
not having a righteousness of my own that comes from the law,
but that which is through faith in Christ–
the righteousness that comes from God and is by faith.
Philippians 3:7–9

Rubbish: Greek, *skubalon* (skoo'-bal-on): what is thrown to the dogs, refuse, dung

Manure, dung, stinking and worthless trash describe Saul's religious accomplishments prior to his encounter with Jesus. Try to imagine the foul, fermented odor Saul carried around with him. Don't be fooled. We smell the same way when we try to impress God by splashing ourselves with performance and perfectionism. Graciously, that which Saul's flesh was never able to accomplish God did–not only for Saul, but for all of us.

. . . until the Seed to whom the promise referred had come.
Galatians 3:19a (emphasis mine)

Today in the town of David a Savior has been born to you;

he is Christ the Lord.
Luke 2:11 (emphasis mine)

"For God so loved the world that he gave his one and only Son . . ."
John 3:16a (emphasis mine)

The sending forth of God's Son brought salvation from the very sins which God's laws had magnified and condemned. But God would not condemn those created in his image without providing the means for their reconciliation. God promised to send a Seed and a Savior for his children, and this promise came to the world in the form of his very own Son, wrapped in swaddling clothes and lying in a manger. A manger is a feeding trough for farm animals. Isn't it touching that God covered himself with the delicate scent of humility in order to do away with the pungent odor of our pride?

"I WILL"

Centuries before the New Covenant would become a reality, God spoke through his prophets and foretold of its coming.

The Lord your God will circumcise your hearts and the hearts of your descendants,
so that you may love him with all your heart and with all your soul, and live.
You will again obey the Lord and follow all his commands I am giving you today.
I will give you a new heart and put a new spirit in you;
I will remove from you your heart of stone and give you a heart of flesh.
And I will put my Spirit in you and move you to
follow my decrees and be careful to keep my laws.
Deuteronomy 30:6, 8; Ezekiel 36:26–27 (emphases mine)

In the Old Covenant, the heart of man was never changed. Man continually saw his sin, year after year was reminded of his sin, yet was without power to have victory over his sin. The beauty of the New Covenant is that in it God *dealt with the heart of man.*

I will give them an undivided heart and put a new spirit in them;
I will remove from them their heart of stone and give them a heart of flesh.
Then they will follow my decrees and be careful to keep my laws.

They will be my people, and I will be their God.
Ezekiel 11:19–20 (emphasis mine)

"I will," says the Lord. Not your laws, not your rituals or traditions, not your performance—they won't change your heart—*I* will change your heart. God takes responsibility for our ability to keep his laws by changing our hearts into hearts that actually want to and are even careful to keep his laws.

<u>Then</u>—*after our hearts have been changed*, when we receive God's love and become one with Christ—that's when we delight in the laws of God. In union with Christ, we give him our nature and we take on his. His laws are now written on our hearts and in our minds.

Think of the contrast. Before coming into covenant with Christ, God's laws were external. They were hard as stone. These laws exposed our wickedness and reminded us of our sins, leaving us frustrated with our inability to satisfy their holy demands.

The purpose of our frustration is to draw us to Christ. Actually, at its basic level, God gave us the Ten Commandments to show us we can't keep them, and that we desperately need a Savior to satisfy both our helplessness and his holiness. Satisfying God's requirement of holiness is something we could never do on our own. That's why God, in his loving mercy, willingly became man in the form of Jesus and took it upon himself to literally cut covenant with himself—insuring a relationship with us that could never be broken.

In the New Covenant, the once external laws of God come alive in the person of the Holy Spirit and are engraved on our hearts and in our minds. We now have an intimate, *internal* relationship with God and his laws. In the New Covenant, God changes our hearts so that his heart's desire becomes our hearts' desire. We want to obey and uphold God's laws, as they are an expression of Christ living in us. And what does Jesus Christ look like?

"Be holy, because I am holy."
1 Peter 1:16b

The highest purpose of the New Covenant is to restore man from his fall in the Garden of Eden back into fellowship with God. This was our intended home: one with God, walking with God in Paradise.

"Do not think that I have come to abolish the Law or the Prophets;
I have not come to abolish them but to fulfill them."
Matthew 5:17

Fulfill: Greek, *pleroo* (play-ro′-o): to abundantly provide for, to entirely accomplish, to complete, to carry out fully

Jesus completed in the New what man could not do for himself in the Old. Jesus' life meshed the holy demands of the law to the forgiving nature of his Father, resulting in a progressive revelation and more accurate representation of God's nature. Let's not be misled, however, by the depth of God's love toward us. Remember that at the center of God's love lies a very straightforward admonition:

You, my brothers, were called to be free.
But do not use your freedom to indulge the sinful nature;
rather, serve one another in love.
The entire law is summed up in a single command:
"Love your neighbor as yourself."
Galatians 5:13–14 (emphasis mine)

Let's review the ultimate purpose of the Ten Commandments.

1. They magnify our sin,
2. showing us our need for a Savior, the purpose being:
3. to lead us to Jesus for salvation by grace, which is when
4. God's commandments are written on our hearts and in our minds, where they
5. train us in holiness, which is summed up in the command to
6. love your neighbor as yourself, which
7. *brings glory to God*, which
8. is why we were created.

"Bring My sons from afar, And My daughters from the ends of the earth–
Everyone who is called by My name, Whom I have created for My glory;
I have formed him, yes, I have made him."
Isaiah 43:6b–7 (NKJV; emphasis mine)

Grace doesn't need the law to secure our salvation. Grace stands complete. However, after salvation, God calls upon the wisdom of his laws to provide safe boundaries wherein we can live and mature in holiness. Maturing in holiness should be the desire of every believer. The benefits of following the commands of God are countless.

When you walk, they will guide you;
when you sleep, they will watch over you;
when you awake, they will speak to you.
For these commands are a lamp, this teaching is a light,
and the corrections of discipline are the way of life.
Proverbs 6:22–23

The fear of the Lord is the beginning of wisdom;
all who follow his precepts have good understanding.
Psalm 111:10a

Great peace have they who love your law,
and nothing can make them stumble
Psalm 119:165

If only you had paid attention to my commands,
your peace would have been like a river,
your righteousness like the waves of the sea.
Isaiah 48:18

God's laws guide us, watch over and speak to us. They are a light for us to follow and they provide us with good understanding. They secure our peace and stability. These are descriptions of a parent loving his child.

A NEW COMMANDMENT

Truly, grace is the power that changes the laws of God from being an ugly reflection of our sins into something entirely new and much more beautiful. So dramatic is the effect of love on these laws that they're hardly recognizable. It's like looking at a butterfly and straining to remember how it looked as a caterpillar.

When we look at the Ten Commandments and sin is defined clearly for us, when we see and are frustrated by our inability to keep these commandments, and then when we ask Jesus to come into our lives to save us from our sins, *that's the point in time when the purpose of God's laws are changed.* This is the moment the laws of God penetrate into our hearts and our minds.

The writer of Hebrews described the effect grace has upon God's laws as being so profound as to render them unrecognizable, to the point of being obsolete (Hebrews 8:13a). Yes, grace causes the *initial purpose* of God's law to be obsolete, but was a butterfly not once a caterpillar? Does the freedom of the butterfly annul the value of the caterpillar? In fact, the beauty of the butterfly should be enhanced by the memory of its former state. To think that the caterpillar (who once crept wearily on its belly) is now endowed with the ability to fly: this is the power grace has upon our hearts and minds—as well as the laws of God. We're changed. The purpose of God's laws has changed. *Grace does that.* We cannot, however, simply discard the law because grace has changed its purpose. Instead, we should appreciate the good news that, when we receive God's grace, his laws change from showing us our need for a Savior to helping us live more intimately with our Savior.

When we accept Christ as our Savior, a powerful blessing occurs. Jesus, in the Person of the Holy Spirit, comes to live within us and assumes responsibility for carrying the demands of the laws that, prior to salvation, were too burdensome for us to bear. God's laws are now written on our hearts and in our minds. Through Christ living in us, our eyes are opened to see the wisdom contained within the Ten Commandments and to delight in obeying them.

By this we know that we love the children of God,
when we love God and keep His commandments.
For this is the love of God, that we keep His commandments.
and His commandments are not burdensome.
1 John 5:2–3 (NKJV; emphases mine)

So, then, what does "the love of God" look like? *The love of God looks like the keeping of his commandments.* And his commandments are . . .

Not burdensome: Greek, *barus* (bar-ooce'): weighty, heavy, grievous; a load

Burdensome denotes "a weight, anything pressing on one physically" (Vine, 83). God's laws are burdensome for the person who doesn't have Christ living in him. However, God's commands are not burdensome "for everyone born of God" (1 John 5:4). God's commands are not burdensome for his children because the power of God, in the Person of the Holy Spirit, is living within them and has changed their hearts, giving them the desire and empowering them to keep God's commandments. Such is the power of grace!

For the law was given through Moses,
but grace and truth came through Jesus Christ.
John 1:17 (NKJV)

Grace: Greek, *charis* (khar'-ece): acceptable; benefit, favor, gift, pleasure; the divine influence upon the heart and its reflection in the life, including gratitude

Sad to say that the grace God so desperately wants to impart to his children is as hard to grasp for the people of today as it was in the early days of the church, when Stephen and Paul were spreading its life-giving message. For many, this free and intimate expression of love is oftentimes viewed as threatening. But for others it's downright refreshing.

"A new commandment I give to you, that you love one another;
as I have loved you, that you also love one another.
By this all will know that you are My disciples, if you have love for one another."
John 13:34–35 (NKJV)

New: Greek, *kainos* (kahee-nos′): not previously known, newly made or obtained, refreshing, additional or further
Commandment: Greek, *entole* (en-tol-ay′): injunction, an authoritative prescription

An injunction is defined as "a judicial process or order requiring the person or persons to whom it is directed to do or refrain from doing a particular act" (*Random House Dictionary*, 686). In other words, if we've received and benefitted from God's love, we're *legally bound* to love others in the same way God has loved us.

Let no debt remain outstanding, except the continuing debt to love one another,
for he who loves his fellowman has fulfilled the law. The commandments,
"Do not commit adultery," "Do not murder," "Do not steal," "Do not covet,"
and whatever other commandment there may be, are summed up in this one rule :
"Love your neighbor as yourself."
Love does not harm to its neighbor.
Therefore love is the fulfillment of the law.
Romans 13:8–10

THE GREATEST COMMANDMENT

It's a mystery how Christ comes to live within our hearts. Words to describe this phenomenon don't exist. The inability to explain this miracle is, however, no fault of the miracle. It does happen.

To them God has chosen to make known among the Gentiles
the glorious riches of this mystery,
which is Christ in you, the hope of glory.
Colossians 1:27 (emphasis mine)

Embodied within the word "in" is a very rich meaning. "In" conveys the idea that Christ is embraced, *moving from outside to a point within.* (Remember how the laws of God changed from being external to internal?) As believers, we carry within our hearts the ability to love, for Christ in the Person of the Holy Spirit now lives and dwells inside us. It's not we who love but Love Himself expressing himself through us, his willing believers. The ability to love is now an outward manifestation of an inward relationship.

What do we do when we move into a used home? We paint the walls a different color, hang pictures, maybe change the carpet, all with the goal of making our home reflect us and our personality. Jesus is the same way. Once he moves inside his new home, he immediately begins to make changes that reflect his personality and are compatible with his character. A litmus test of true salvation will be the activity of Christ moving around in our lives. As believers, spiritual activity, good works, changes in our lives and behavior are pleasing to God, as they point to Jesus and the effect he is having in our lives. James, the brother of our Lord, had this concept in mind when he wrote:

In the same way, faith by itself, if it is not accompanied by action, is dead.
But someone will say, "You have faith; I have deeds."
Show me your faith without deeds,
and <u>I will show you my faith by what I do</u>.
You believe there is one God. Good!
Even the demons believe that–and shudder.
James 2:17–19 (emphasis mine)

James is speaking in the context of doing good works and how works relate to our faith in Christ. We can do all kinds of good works in our communities and even in our churches and still not believe *in* Christ. We can believe there is one God. So what? Demons believe there is one God, and, to their credit (if that can even be plausible), they shudder.

Good works point to one of two places: faith in ourselves or faith in God. Good works prior to believing in Christ didn't save James or Paul, and they won't save you or me. However, good works after we ask Jesus to be our Savior are expressions of Christ living in us. Not only will good works follow our faith in Christ, but *wanting to live by the laws of God will be a natural expression of Christ living in us.*

Hearing that Jesus had silenced the Sadducees, the Pharisees got together.
One of them, an expert in the law, tested him with this question:
"Teacher, which is the greatest commandment in the Law?"
Jesus replied: " 'Love the Lord your God with all your heart and with all your soul
and with all your mind.' This is the first and <u>greatest</u> commandment.
And the second is like it: 'Love your neighbor as yourself.'
All the Law and the prophets hang on these two commandments."
Matthew 22:34–40 (emphasis mine)

TEST TIME

Examine yourselves to see whether you are in the faith;
test yourselves.
Do you not realize that Christ Jesus is in you–
unless, of course, you fail the test?
2 Corinthians 13:5

Examine: Greek, *peirazo* (pi-rad'-zo): to scrutinize, to prove, to test

I recall my days of taking tests. I didn't like them, but I never took a test lightly. I would study and make notes, memorize important facts and even write out a mock test to take before being examined. After I'd completed the exam, I'd carefully review my answers, making sure I was as accurate as possible.

To scrutinize something is to give it a very close inspection. It involves looking something over again and again, in a very critical manner. Examining whether or not we're truly in the faith is worthy of such an inspection. Why? Because the very destiny of our souls is at stake.

And everyone who calls on the name of the Lord will be saved.
Acts 2:21

Saved: Greek, *sozo* (sode'-zo): delivered, healed, protected, preserved

Have you been delivered from your sin? Are you healed, protected, and preserved for all eternity to live with the Lord? I'm not asking if you've joined a church, walked down a church aisle, been baptized, taught Sunday School or even pastored a church. You may have done all these things, but never had a true *change of heart*.

Let's ask ourselves a couple more questions: "What do we believe about believing? What does it mean to 'be a believer in Christ'?" Perhaps our understanding of "belief" can be strengthened by focusing on a person who lived a life of belief. We'll recall that belief paved the way for Abraham to leave his homeland and travel to a country he'd never seen. For Abraham, believing was a verb.

What does the Scripture say?
"Abraham believed God,
and it was credited to him as righteousness."
Romans 4:3

Believed: Greek, *pisteuo* (pist-yoo'-o): to have faith in a person, to entrust one's well-being to Christ; reliance upon Christ for salvation

We must be accurate in our understanding of what it means to "believe there is a God" versus what it means to "believe in God" (we're taking a test, after all, and there's an eternal nuance between the two). Satan does not entrust his well-being to God or rely on God's Son for his righteousness. While Satan believes there *is* a God, he does not believe *in* God.

It requires faith to believe in a God who loved us from the beginning of time. It takes faith to believe God loved us before we performed any good works or were able to obey or disobey any of his commandments. God loved us before we were even born. That's right. He loved us when he spoke the heavens and earth into existence. Next, he created light for us to live by, air for us to breathe, water to drink, land to walk upon, food to eat and animals to enjoy. God provided everything Adam needed before he created Adam. He even provided the means for mankind's salvation from the foundations of the earth.

All inhabitants of the earth will worship the beast–
all whose names have not been written in the book of life
belonging to the Lamb that was slain from the creation of the world.
He who has an ear, let him hear.
Revelation 13:8–9a (emphasis mine)

We were in God's thoughts when he knelt to the ground, formed Adam from the dust of the earth and breathed into Adam the breath of life. God knew all about us during the days of Abraham, Isaac, and Jacob. It was for our benefit that God gave Moses The Ten Commandments, to clarify what sin is and cause us to *realize our need for a Savior.* God doesn't want to judge us by the standard of his holy laws (he knows we would all fall short). Rather, he wants us to rejoice in the knowledge that the judgment of these laws has been *covered with mercy and sprinkled with the blood of his Son.* God loves us! Oh, that we may understand that the highest purpose of The Ten Commandments is to bring us to this love.

Love One Another

PRINCIPLES

1. In the New Covenant, God's laws are written on our hearts and in our minds.
2. When we unite our lives with Christ, the purpose of the law changes from showing us our sins to helping us live closer to our Savior.
3. At salvation, our hearts change into hearts that delight in doing God's will.
4. God's commands are not burdensome for the believer because the Holy Spirit is empowering him to keep God's commands.
5. It's natural for Jesus, living in us, to want to uphold the laws of his Father.
6. Grace finished what the law began.
7. Believing that God's Son died for our sins is the *only* means whereby our salvation is secured (Acts 4:12).
8. Religious people are often threatened by God's grace and power.
9. Evidence of Christ living in us is the presence of spiritual activity.

Love One Another

DISCUSSION QUESTIONS

1. What motivated Abram to ask Sarai to lie about their relationship?
2. In what area of your life are you most vulnerable to defeat?
3. Can you identify a wound in your past which contributed to being vulnerable in this specific area?
4. Determine the commandment(s) you feel God wants to strengthen into your life.
5. How would you answer if a friend asked you: "Why did God give us the Ten Commandments?"
6. Why do you think "power" and "grace" were such threats to the Sanhedrin?
7. Why do you think the commandment to love one another should have been refreshing to our spiritual forefathers?
8. How does it feel, knowing a Savior was provided for you before the foundations of the world? (Revelation 13:8)
9. Why is it more difficult to keep God's commandments before you believe in Christ as opposed to after you've believed in Christ?
10. What are some practical ways you want a specific commandment to impact your life?
11. Why is keeping the commandments of God evidence of loving him? (1 John 5:2–5)
12. Why is it important to God that Christians love one another?

REFERENCES

Barker, Kenneth, ed. *New International Version Study Bible*, Red Letter Edition. Grand Rapids, MI: Zondervan Bible Publishers, 1984.

Freeman, James M. *Manners and Customs*. Rewritten and updated by Harold J. Chadwick. North Brunswick, NJ: Bridge-Logos Publishers, 1998.

Matthews, Kyle. http://www.kylematthews.com.

Strong, James, S.T.D., LL.D. *Strong's Exhaustive Concordance of the Bible with Hebrew and Greek Dictionaries*. McLean, VA: MacDonald Publishing Company, n.d.

Urdang, Laurence, ed. *The Random House Dictionary*. New York: Random House, Inc., 1973.

Vine, W. E. *Vine's Complete Expository Dictionary*. Nashville, TN: Thomas Nelson Publishers, 1996.

Willmington, Harold L., D. Min., ed. *The Open Bible New King James Version*, Nashville, TN: Thomas Nelson Publishers, 1997.

ABOUT THE AUTHOR

Pat Menser

Pat grew up in Kentucky, moved to Georgia, and now lives in Charlotte, NC with her husband of nearly 40 years. Pat holds degrees from Luther Rice Bible College and Western Kentucky University. She has taught Bible studies for over thirty years and is presently serving as a Care Minister at Grace Covenant Church in Cornelius, NC. Pat enjoys traveling with her husband and spending time with their grandchildren (and children too, of course!).

CPSIA information can be obtained
at www.ICGtesting.com
Printed in the USA
FSOW03n0348120217
30631FS